What people are sayin…

You Die at the F…
Mortality and th…

Rarely do you read someone sp… you in the second person. Only those in your circle a… …lowed to address you on that level, and probe your feelings and emotions. Dr. Ferraiolo comes right at you, as if at a table for two, you and he, getting personal. He is into your stuff. Yet you are not intimidated or put off; you do not resent his sudden immediacy. He shows no cockiness, no swagger. He urges you to work harder, but you feel no resentment. He is direct, he does not waste words, yet his prose is gentle, light–but not flippant. He brings no fierceness, he does not preach… or sell. You listen. He tells you about the giants whose high shoulders offer a new vantage. He is not above you nor better than you; he is a fellow traveler.
Tim McGarvey, author, *Only the Days We Danced*

Like Lady Macbeth, I had to "screw my courage to the sticking place," put on my hair shirt and cilice and take my punishment—modern sinner that I am. This work is no *Book of Common Prayer*, no visual "diamond" of St. Teresa of Avila's "interior castle." Instead, these daily meditations demand a hard look at one's frailties and a hard shove toward remedy. Ferraiolo pulls no punches, and now bloodied, I am to regard my trouncing as veritable proof of life's purpose—to make of suffering, a life of gratitude.
Paula Sheil, Tuleburg Press

William Ferraiolo is a wise philosopher. I enjoyed his interview on my podcast, and got to learn about his fascinating story and unique perspectives on life. He has learned a lot about human

nature and about morals. I liked hearing about his approach to Stoicism and how similar it is to the lessons of non-attachment from the Buddha. I would recommend his book, *You Die at the End: Meditations on Mortality and the Human Condition*, to anyone looking to learn more about the purpose of life, and how to conduct themselves with respect and honor.
Jake Guy, host of Mindset Coaching Podcast

You Die at the End

Meditations on Mortality and the Human Condition

You Die at the End

Meditations on Mortality and the Human Condition

William Ferraiolo

BOOKS

Winchester, UK
Washington, USA

JOHN HUNT PUBLISHING

First published by O-Books, 2020
O-Books is an imprint of John Hunt Publishing Ltd., 3 East St., Alresford,
Hampshire SO24 9EE, UK
office@jhpbooks.com
www.johnhuntpublishing.com
www.o-books.com

For distributor details and how to order please visit the 'Ordering' section on our website.

ISBN: 978 1 78904 393 8
978 1 78904 394 5 (ebook)
Library of Congress Control Number: 2019938349

A CIP catalogue record for this book is available from the British Library.

Design: Stuart Davies

UK: Printed and bound by CPI Group (UK) Ltd, Croydon, CR0 4YY
US: Printed and bound by Thomson-Shore, 7300 West Joy Road, Dexter, MI 48130

Contents

Dedicated to People of the Book

I wish to express my gratitude to *everyone* at John Hunt Publishing, and everyone who has ever tolerated me.

Introduction

You may have heard that the world is a rough place, and no one gets out alive. This seems to be an accurate claim. In the grand scheme of things, you will be dead fairly soon. The world is going to kill you. Between now and then, you might want to think about who you are, what you are doing, and what, if anything, makes your life worth living. It is advisable to find a compelling reason to persist through this "vale of tears." Without such a reason, a hollow feeling at your core tends to develop and ripen. Friedrich Nietzsche said, "He who has a *why* to live can bear almost any *how*." Conversely, without a *why*, a reason to persist, you will find it very difficult to determine *how* to go on. Reality is going to kick your teeth in time and time again. You *will* get knocked down repeatedly. When that happens, and it will happen over and over, you had better find a reason to get back up. Otherwise, *down* is where you will stay. Do you *want* to stay down?

Scripture has served humanity as *one* source of wisdom and inspiration for ages. An excerpt from the Bible accompanies each meditation in this book, and touches on a topic that is either directly or obliquely related to the subject around which the meditation centers. This should not be interpreted as an endorsement, or as a rejection, of the Bible passage quoted in each case or of the lesson contained therein. This approach is merely a matter of this author ruminating about elements of the human condition that were sufficiently interesting to make their way into scripture. The fundamentals of a human life on this planet have not changed so very much over the millennia. The world is large and indifferent to the suffering of its denizens, its inhabitants. Perhaps there is a God who is *not* indifferent. Perhaps there is no such God. There *are*, however, people who suffer. Those people sometimes wonder about their suffering, their place in this world, and (forgive the expression) God knows what else. Indeed, the feelings of confusion, frustration, and various forms of psychological and emotional suffering are nearly ubiquitous elements of the human enterprise. Ignorance about such matters is *not* bliss. This is one author's attempt to contemplate a few elements of the human condition from the perspective of an individual, middling effort to manage a human life. Perhaps this will prove worthy of the reader's time and effort. The author hopes to be of service. The author frequently fails. Sometimes, the author blunders into a brief, useful moment of clarity. Read on to find out if this book serves as a useful blunder. Thank you for giving the author's work a chance.

January

1In the beginning God created the heavens and the earth.

2Now the earth was formless and void, and darkness was over
the surface of the deep. And the Spirit of God was hovering
over the surface of the waters.

The First Day

3And God said, "Let there be light," and there was light. 4And
seeing that the light was good, God separated the light from
the darkness. 5God called the light "day," and the darkness
He called "night."

And there was evening, and there was morning—the first day.

Genesis 1

Might this not serve as an allusion, for pre-scientific humanity, to what contemporary cosmologists refer to as the Big Bang? From darkness, from a close cousin of nothingness, from a space-time singularity, a burst of electromagnetic energy of unimaginable scale sets the cosmos in motion. Surely, one can be forgiven for imagining God as the first, uncaused cause of the Big Bang and all that has followed. Perhaps, one can equally be forgiven for struggling mightily, and failing, to imagine any viable alternative. It may be that an alternative explanation awaits discovery. You are hereby absolved of the "sin" of doubting that a viable naturalistic explanation hides just beyond the current scientific horizons. Suspicions of something transcendent, something other than natural law, something other than matter and energy, are entirely reasonable. Those who use "faith" as a pejorative are free to do so. You need not concern yourself with their beliefs. They are as entitled to theirs as you are to yours.

Let them be. Stand in God's light, and learn what you can about the human condition. If God does not exist, then the irreligious are correct. Well, bully for them. For now, it seems we have no choice but to place our bets and live accordingly. There *is* something rather than nothing. We *are* here. It did not *have* to be so. Why are *you* here? The speculation is worth at least a bit of your time, is it not?

1 Then the LORD answered Job out of the whirlwind and said:

2 "Who is this who obscures My counsel
by words without knowledge?
3 Now brace yourself like a man;
I will question you, and you shall inform Me!
4 Where were you when I laid the foundations of the earth?
Tell Me, if you have understanding.
5 Who fixed its measurements? Surely you know!
Or who stretched a measuring line across it?
6 On what were its foundations laid,
or who set its core in place—
7 while the morning stars sang together
and all the sons of God shouted for joy?"

Job 38

God does not owe Job an explanation. He owes none of us, whether He exists or not, any explanation for anything. The world is as He will have it, or the world is as it is in the absence of intelligent guidance or cosmological engineering. We suffer. What of it? We experience disappointment. Where is the blame properly laid for that? Nothing compels your expectations beyond the confines of your own mind, and the guidance of your cognitive apparatus. If you have allowed yourself to expect events that did not transpire, do not blame the world, and do not blame events, for failing to satisfy your expectations. Events owe you nothing. The world need not conform to your desires. Neither the world, nor its author (if it *has* an author) owes you a thing. No promises were made, no contract was signed, and no offer was extended. You simply "woke up" in this
was not necessary. Counterfactual worlds in which
no appearance are legion—if not infinite. Do you su
of the world as it stands? Do you complain of you

Who are *you* that you pass judgment against reality and gripe about the way of things? Where were you when the firmament exploded into being? You were not even dust. It is to less than dust that you shall return. Try not to complain along the journey. Try not to make a nuisance of yourself.

10 Luxury is unseemly for a fool—
how much worse for a slave to rule over princes!

11 A man's insight gives him patience,
and his virtue is to overlook an offense.

12 A king's rage is like the roar of a lion,
but his favor is like dew on the grass.

13 A foolish son is his father's ruin,
and a quarrelsome wife is like a constant dripping.

14 Houses and wealth are inherited from fathers,
but a prudent wife is from the LORD.

Proverbs 19

What, at this very moment, is your primary concern, and what is the object of your current focus and energies? If you aim at anything other than improving yourself, pause and reflect upon the value of the enterprise in which you find yourself currently engaged. What urge do you seek to satisfy, apart from the urge to become a better and wiser person? Is the satisfaction of that urge more valuable than increasing your wisdom and attaining greater mastery of your character and behavior? Give a name to this alternative achievement that allegedly outstrips the merit of improving yourself as best you are able. If you can name it, and if it is a superior expenditure of your vital energies, then get about it. Be sure, however, that you do not merely join the masses in their collective dissolution and heedlessness of their proper moral purpose. Take care that you do not become what you have beheld with disdain and contempt. Do not join in petty amusement and self-abasement, unless mere survival and comfort strike you as noble goals. If, on the other hand, you reckon that you have the fortitude for pursuing nobility, then desist in small-minded endeavors. Such projects tend to diminish those who indulge in them, do they not? To diminish oneself is a proper goal only for those to whom enlargement of spirit seems too tall a task for the undertaking. Which type *do* you think you are? The question is entirely in earnest. What is it that you wish to become? If the goal is ennobling, get to it with all of your strength, every iota of resolve you can muster, and every hope that is worthy of a rational agent. Get to work.

16 Do not be overly righteous, and do not make yourself
too wise. Why should you destroy yourself? 17 Do not be
excessively wicked, and do not be a fool. Why should you die
before your time? 18 It is good to grasp the one and not let the
other slip from your hand. For he who fears God will follow
both warnings.

19 Wisdom makes the wise man
stronger than ten rulers in a city.
20 Surely there is no righteous man on earth
who does good and never sins.

Ecclesiastes 7

If there were a God, would He approve of you? Of course, there may well *be* a God, and He may well *disapprove* of you, your values, your actions, and He may regard your life as a befouling of His creation. How confident can you be of the contrary? *For* you, the world may well have been made, and *on* you, this gift may have been wasted. Are you certain that it is not so? Do you, at least, hope that you are not frittering away a gift beyond measure? Show the accomplishments you have managed with the meager abilities with which you have been endowed and entrusted. Display your greatest and most essential contribution to the unfolding, evolving story of humanity and its struggles. Hold your life up as your "work of art," your addition to the ongoing enterprise that is the world (possibly God's world), and stand proudly beneath it. Show yourself! Is the prospect of doing so invigorating, or does it terrify you? A bit of chill makes its way up your spine just now, does it not? How much time you have had, and how little you have achiev
time. What a waste. What a shame. Perhaps, your
at an end. Perhaps, a long life still lies ahead. T
remains is not up to you. Your use of that time is an

altogether. What excuse do you offer for the life you have lived thus far? Should you not at least hope that some excuse might present itself? If not, you had better hope for sufficient time and opportunity to reverse course and make something of the life that remains. If *this* is the best you can manage, hang your head and know that you have thrown away the only opportunity you are likely to experience. What a waste. What a shame.

1This is an oracle concerning the Desert by the Sea:

Like whirlwinds sweeping through the Negev,
an invader comes from the desert, from a land of terror.
2A dire vision is declared to me:
"The traitor still betrays,
and the destroyer still destroys.
Go up, O Elam! Lay siege, O Media!
I will put an end to all her groaning."

3Therefore my body is filled with anguish.
Pain grips me, like the pains of a woman in labor.
I am bewildered to hear,
I am dismayed to see.
4My heart staggers;
fear makes me tremble.
The twilight of my desire
has turned to horror.

Isaiah 21

The nagging aches and recurring pains have become so familiar that you struggle to remember what life was like without them. Your back and neck sometimes feel better rather than worse, but neither is ever *good*. Neither affords you comfort or confidence that your body will not fail you at some crucial moment. Your knees, even on good days, seem like evidence of a design flaw, shoddy workmanship, or a practical joke. A weak hinge joint on the lower half of a bipedal mammal is a mockery of evolutionary adaptation. How did your ancestors survive the brutality of a pre-civilized world with this haphazard hodgepodge of contrivances masquerading as a well-adapted, functioning unity? Yours is a species of weaklings with delusions of grandeur—born of wet, gray meat sloshing about in a thin layer of fluid separating it from a bony skull that has proven all too fragile on all too many occasions. You could add to this list of bodily inadequacies *ad nauseam* (almost literally). What would the act of producing and enumerating such a list profit you? Whining is a pathetic weakling's response to difficulties, and a waste of your time. Stop! Drag that carcass wherever you must, by whatever means necessary, and get about the business of decency and honor. Griping is a poor method for the purpose.

7The memory of the righteous is a blessing,
but the name of the wicked will rot.

8A wise heart will receive commandments,
but foolish lips will come to ruin.

9He who walks in integrity walks securely,
but he who perverts his ways will be found out.

10He who winks the eye causes grief,
and foolish lips will come to ruin.

11The mouth of the righteous is a fountain of life,
but the mouth of the wicked conceals violence.

12Hatred stirs up dissension,
but love covers all transgressions.

13Wisdom is found on the lips of the discerning,
but a rod is for the back of him who lacks judgment.

Proverbs 10

You often want nothing to do with your fellow talking primates, and you often struggle to repress the urge to let them hear and feel your contempt in no uncertain terms. Of course, you are no better than the rest of humanity at large. You have no illusions about this. You are not *better*; you are simply disinclined to share more moments, more energy, more of your limited vitality, with others than is a matter of practical necessity. You understand other people even less than you understand yourself. They seem to understand you at least as poorly as you understand them. The chasm between you and nearly everyone else you encounter seems impossible to bridge—and unworthy of the requisite effort. You must let go of any final vestiges of the urge to be understood or embraced. Are you wiser or more virtuous if someone applauds your work, or seeks to embrace you, or claims to share with you some "common ground" upon which your minds may meet and mutually appreciate each other? Leave them all be. Go your own way. Let them go theirs. Turn away, and ignore the chattering behind you.

29 If these things are not so, what will those do who are
baptized for the dead? If the dead are not raised at all, why
are people baptized for them? 30 And why do we endanger
ourselves every hour? 31 I face death every day, brothers, as
surely as I boast about you in Christ Jesus our Lord. 32 If I
fought wild beasts in Ephesus for human motives, what did I
gain? If the dead are not raised,

"Let us eat and drink,
for tomorrow we die."

33 Do not be deceived: "Bad company corrupts good character."
34 Sober up as you ought, and stop sinning; for some of you are
ignorant of God. I say this to your shame.

1 Corinthians 15

Oh, how you despise all blather about "the common good" and related, meaningless euphemisms. This poisonous abstraction has been used to justify every form of communalist stupidity and anti-individualist gibberish imaginable—and surely more tripe will be concocted in defense of the herd mentality. You are *not* some trivial component of an amorphous, infinitely malleable aggregate of humanity in its odoriferous generality. *Never* embrace any belief, any proposition, any habit, or any part of any worldview merely because you are an alleged part of some supposedly "greater" whole. Secede from any collective that is, by your lights, ignoble, silly, or otherwise unworthy of your allegiance. You need not await anyone's permission to do so. No mass movement is required. You need not convince anyone else to join your egress. There are no required forms, applications, or petitions necessary. Turn your back and walk away from anyone and anything that stakes illegitimate claims upon you, your allegiance, or your time and energy. Scrape it off. Drop it in your wake. Waste not one more thought on the "common," but pursue only the *good*. Those who do not share this goal are unworthy of your company, or even your notice. Their fate is nothing to you. Take no notice of snails.

9The coming of the lawless one will be accompanied by the
working of Satan, with every kind of power, sign, and false
wonder, 10and with every wicked deception directed against
those who are perishing, because they refused the love of
the truth that would have saved them. 11For this reason, God
will send them a powerful delusion so that they will believe
the lie, 12in order that judgment will come upon all who have
disbelieved the truth and delighted in wickedness.

2 Thessalonians 2

Politicians pander to the credulous masses. Do you blame the politicians for this? How so? Can one win election to any significant office by telling the truth, the whole truth, and nothing but the truth? The truth about *oneself* is usually sufficiently off-putting to darken any conversation, and would surely serve to forestall the average voter's support. How much less felicitous would be the naked, unadorned articulation of the truth about the masses themselves, accurate accounting of future prospects for the nation, the economy, the environment, and the likelihood of warfare and terrorism? Who will cast a vote for the politician who publicly declares that the average voter is an ignoramus, and that political speeches must be delivered so that an addled adolescent mind might find the speech agreeable and comprehensible? A democracy is rarely more virtuous than the voters who select their leaders. Hence, democracy is doomed to an ignominious persistence—unto death and collapse. A tyranny of an obnoxious, oppressive, or moronic majority is a tyranny nonetheless, and ought to be resisted as much as is possible, and also borne with rational, detached indifference in all of those manifestations that lie beyond your capacity to resist. If you find yourself in agreement with the majority, do not interpret *that* as evidence that you are correct, or that the issue in question is either settled or otherwise uncontroversial. Facts are not subject to plebiscite. The truth is not determined by taking a survey. Think for yourself. *Govern* yourself. Do not enslave yourself to the whims of the majority.

20 Then Job stood up, tore his robe, and shaved his head. He
fell to the ground and worshiped, 21 saying:

"Naked I came from my mother's womb,
and naked I shall return.
The LORD gave, and the LORD has taken away.
Blessed be the name of the LORD."

22 In all this, Job did not sin or charge God with wrongdoing.

Job 1

If this experience is "too much" for you, then know that you are too little for this experience. Do you dare declare yourself unable to shoulder a burden that has been borne before, under far less favorable circumstances, by those with far less wherewithal than is available to you? Coward! Weakling! Lie down and die, you useless bag of flesh. Either that, or stand up and face the challenge before you like a warrior, and leave all complaints among the childish things you should have put away a long time ago. You wish to respect yourself, do you not? If so, rise to this challenge and decide that you will die before you will allow yourself to yield, before you will allow yourself to break psychologically or emotionally. Anything less is pusillanimous and degrading. If servility suits you, start crawling. Behave like a recalcitrant dog being dragged by a leash. If you voluntarily enslave yourself, then kneel to the "master" at the business end of the whip. This is not hyperbole. You are not any less subservient than canines crawling on their bellies if you allow circumstances to dictate your attitude, your mood, and to induce discreditable behavior and utterances. Your fear is greater than your courage, is it? Die then. Make room for those who refuse to be broken. There are still some persons who live like rocks against which the waves of life's vicissitudes break. Are *you* a rock? Prove it, or shatter. Leave the whimpering to those who can manage no better.

12He pulled down the altars that the kings of Judah had set up
on the roof near the upper chamber of Ahaz, and the altars
Manasseh had set up in the two courtyards of the house of the
LORD. The king pulverized them there and threw their dust
into the Kidron Valley.

13The king also desecrated the high places east of Jerusalem,
to the south of the Mount of Corruption, which King Solomon
of Israel had built for Ashtoreth the abomination of the
Sidonians, for Chemosh the abomination of the Moabites, and
for Molech the abomination of the Ammonites. 14He smashed
the sacred pillars to pieces, cut down the Asherah poles, and
covered the sites with human bones.

2 Kings 23

Complaining about corruption is a bit like complaining about gravity, is it not? The latter, to be sure, is a law of nature, but the former is not terribly far removed from the realm of physical necessity. Lord Acton told us "power corrupts," and mentioned an "absolute" in conjunction with that dictum. He was not wrong, was he? You have encountered *very* few persons occupying positions of power, or lusting after such positions, or esteem, or fame, who do so with pure hearts and pristine intentions. Perhaps the causal arrow is presented in reverse, though. It may be that only those who are inherently corrupt prove susceptible to the desire to wield power over others. Perhaps the virtuous few are content to govern their own character and behavior, and to leave the realms of politics and business to the devices and artifices of others. Had you ever been afforded the opportunity to wield power over others, what might you have done with it? Can you not imagine yourself misusing your station? Do not even lean in the direction of that delusion. You are *not* to trust yourself with that kind of power. Do *not* pursue it. Cleave to what meager virtues you may have. Do not sacrifice the little progress you have made. Maintain *some* dignity. If you fail to do so, and you attribute your failure to the misdeeds or the corruption of the "powers that be," you are guilty of a dual perversion. Do not hand your self-governance over to other persons, and then complain about the manner in which those other persons treat you. *You* are responsible for your character.

10 The workers in cloth will be dejected,
and all the wage earners will be sick at heart. 11 The princes of
Zoan are mere fools;

Pharaoh's wise counselors give senseless advice.
How can you say to Pharaoh,
"I am one of the wise,
a son of eastern kings"? 12 Where are your wise men now?
Let them tell you and reveal
what the LORD of Hosts
has planned against Egypt.

Isaiah 19

Who are *you* that you presume to share your thoughts with others? How perverse is this act in which you are currently engaged? You hold your words up to the world as if anyone, anywhere, ought to care about *anything* that you have *ever* had to say. There is hubris in that. In your case, it is entirely unearned. Look at the wreckage that is your internal life, your muddy and contaminated stream of consciousness. To whom are you qualified to offer advice? Even Socrates refrained from holding himself up as an idol for emulation. You are certainly *no* Socrates! Indeed, you are not even the equal of a Meletus, Anytus, or Lycon—who had Socrates martyred to the cause of philosophy, inquiry, and the pursuit of wisdom. What have *you* accomplished in the name of philosophy? At least those miscreants had a good man executed so that posterity could not forget his life and his deeds. You, on the other hand, have done about as much for posterity as posterity has done for you. Is this twaddle your contribution? Is *this* the best that you can do? If not, get to work on producing better and more ennobling work. If, however, this *is* your "great contribution" to humanity, then your life is as sad a story as is this peculiar tale that you currently tell. Something of a pickle, is it not? If you have something worthwhile to communicate about noble character, it ought to be apparent in your conduct. If you feel the need to *explain* decency, it may be that you fail to *embody* it properly.

23All this I tested by wisdom, saying, "I resolve to be wise."
But it was beyond me. 24What exists is out of reach and very
deep. Who can fathom it?

25I directed my mind to understand, to explore, to search out
wisdom and explanations, and to understand the stupidity of
wickedness and the folly of madness. 26And I find more bitter
than death the woman who is a snare, whose heart is a net,
and whose hands are chains. The man who pleases God will
escape her, but the sinner will be ensnared.

Ecclesiastes 7

The cultural decay and degeneration proceeds apace, or so it would seem. Incompetence has become so common, so pervasive, and so intense, that its absence causes you surprise and a perverse sort of disappointment. Competence and diligence have a slightly disorienting effect. How does anything get accomplished anywhere? Moreover, how is it that *you* ever accomplish anything? Face the facts. You are at least as much of an imbecile as those you encounter as you stumble and bumble through your day. Is it possible that just living in the dying West is sufficient to dull your cognitive faculties? Jesus told his followers that the poor would always be with us, but he declined to mention the idiots. Surely, there are more of those than there are persons living in poverty. The wealthy have plenty of nitwits among their number. Where is the charitable organization devoted to stamping out idiocy in our time? No "race for the cure" is worthy in this arena? Baffling. Perhaps stupidity is incorrigibly resistant to all human efforts to cure or manage it. It may well be that humanity is doomed in this regard. After all, this condition may not be particularly unjust. Why does the human race *not* deserve to suffer the consequences of the rampant, broadly distributed stupidity of its members? Being stupid is hazardous to your health, and detrimental to the well-being of the species, not to mention other conscious, sentient creatures. What did you expect from billions of talking, vaguely psychotic apes? We cannot all be the equivalent of Moses or Shakespeare. You are ample proof of that, are you not?

7 For you yourselves know how you ought to imitate us,
because we were not undisciplined among you, 8 nor did
we eat anyone's food without paying for it. Instead, in
labor and toil, we worked night and day so that we would
not be a burden to any of you. 9 Not that we lack this right,
but we wanted to offer ourselves as an example for you to
imitate. 10 For even while we were with you, we gave you this
command: "If anyone is unwilling to work, he shall not eat."

11 Yet we hear that some of you are leading undisciplined
lives and accomplishing nothing but being busybodies. 12 We
command and urge such people by our Lord Jesus Christ to
begin working quietly to earn their own living. 13 But as for
you, brothers, do not grow weary in well-doing.

2 Thessalonians 3

There is work to be done, and you have no business calling yourself an adult if you disdain the work that needs doing. Never look down your nose at a job that requires getting dirty, or immersing yourself in environments that most avoid. A virtuous plumber is no less virtuous for working in sewage, and with the apparatus for moving it about. A virtuous plumber is certainly no less virtuous than is a vicious politician, a crooked banker, or a corrupt business mogul. A skilled carpenter with a happy spouse and family presents far greater evidence of decency than does a celebrity behaving like a child, while their spouse and children look on aghast and suffer needlessly because the "big shot" is addicted to fame. When work presents itself to be done, get about the business of doing it immediately and without complaint. If the job to be done is too much for you, then admit that you are too little for it—and hide your head. Consider the herculean efforts of your forebears, of those who erected massive monuments, of those who built empires, or those who managed to produce works of art that have astonished and inspired the people who have been fortunate enough to encounter them up close and in person. Can you not muster sufficient fortitude to manage far, *far* lesser endeavors and achievements? How very sad. How very pathetic.

18 If men are quarreling and one strikes the other with a stone
or a fist, and he does not die but is confined to bed, 19 then
the one who struck him shall go unpunished, as long as the
other can get up and walk around outside with his staff.
Nevertheless, he must compensate the man for his lost work
and see that he is completely healed.

20 If a man strikes his manservant or maidservant with a rod,
and the servant dies by his hand, he shall surely be punished.
21 However, if the servant gets up after a day or two, the owner
shall not be punished, since the servant is his property.

Exodus 21

Other persons are free to think what they will and, for the most part, to say and do what they will—provided they do not impinge upon the rights and liberties of their fellow citizens of the world. All of that is precisely *none* of your business, and all of your attempts to peer into the "hearts and minds" of other persons is worse than a waste of time and energy. There is something perverse about the goings-on in question here. The cognitive states experienced by persons other than yourself are not directly subject to your faculty of deliberation and choice—your *will*. What is your *aim* in this bizarre and impotent effort to be clairvoyant or telepathic? What a shame to waste your limited time and energy on endeavors that *cannot* bear fruit. Direct your attention to *your* mental states, the rectification of *your* character, and *your* habits of thought and behavior. Are *your* inadequacies not enough to keep you occupied? This simply cannot be. Consider the temerity necessary to regard the faults, foibles, and flaws of others as more worthy of your attention than your own massive and glaring shortcomings. You are like a petulant child, stamping your feet and griping that everyone around you lacks self-control. So, are you going to throw a fit because of it? How mature. When were you appointed Governor of the Masses? When were you relieved of your duty to govern *your own* behavior? Consider the needless frustration that ensues due to this obsession with other persons and their (alleged) defects of character. Focus where your attention might do some good.

37 Babylon will become a heap of rubble,
a haunt of jackals,
an object of horror and scorn,
without inhabitant.
38 They will roar together like young lions;
they will growl like lion cubs.
39 While they are flushed with heat,
I will serve them a feast,
and I will make them drunk
so that they may revel;
then they will fall asleep forever and never wake up,
declares the LORD.
40 I will bring them down like lambs to the slaughter,
like rams with male goats.

Jeremiah 51

A lamb cannot be trained to be a lion, or even to function as a vague facsimile of the noble "King of the Jungle." All efforts to lionize a lamb are, at best, quixotic endeavors and, at worst, perverse exercises in idiocy. Unfortunately, lions *can* be tamed to behave like submissive, pathetic, servile lambs. If taming a noble beast, and turning it into the equivalent of a house pet is not, in some sense, a *sin,* your understanding of prowess and flourishing is defective indeed. Lion tamers are doing the world a terrible disservice. What is the good of training the powerful to behave after the fashion of the weak, the timid, or those that serve primarily as prey upon which the predators sustain themselves? There are natural warriors among us, without whom the rest of the population would be helpless and subject to the will of those who seek to destroy them. Those who seek to "tame" the natural warriors among us, do the entire population one of the greatest disservices imaginable. Rough beasts serve purposes to which the gentle cannot even aspire. Are you more lion, more lamb, or are you genuinely uncertain about your level of domestication? That last possibility may be the saddest of the available options. Lions *know* that they are lions.

February

28 You must not make any cuts in your bodies for the dead or put tattoo marks on yourselves. I am the LORD.

29 You must not defile your daughter by making her a prostitute, or the land will be prostituted and filled with depravity.

30 You must keep My Sabbaths and have reverence for My sanctuary. I am the LORD.

Leviticus 19

What is the great advantage in being "well-adjusted" to a historical epoch and a culture that exhibit depravity, weakness, and stupidity at nearly every turn? Do you hope to "fit in" among miscreants, liars, cowards, and sheep? Is it your goal to be embraced by moral lepers, charlatans, and people that you would never allow into your home? If not, this culture and this age have precious few spaces allotted for your like. You were, perhaps, "born out of time," but this is not to be used as an excuse for despair, disgust, or surrender. Perhaps some part of you hopes to sustain a level of conviviality irrespective of the character exhibited by your fellow "citizens of the world." Perhaps you hope to "get along" with those whom you encounter irrespective of their behavior or their values and beliefs. What a shame if this is so. If you are willing to trade away your decency for the companionship of scoundrels, then you have found "your people" indeed. You are a member of a tribe of contemptible louts. By all means, go and "flock together" with the repugnant birds of that despicable feather—but retain, at least, the decency to be ashamed of yourself for it. Shame is an underappreciated tool with which to keep your life on the narrow path, and to remind yourself to shun the all too common path to self-destruction. Go chasing after the bright, shiny things like an addle-minded brat, but abandon the pretense that you seek wisdom or virtue. Go find a red rubber ball and bounce it. Go find yourself a lollipop, moron.

5 No longer will a fool be called noble,
nor a scoundrel said to be important.
6 For a fool speaks foolishness;
his mind plots iniquity.
He practices ungodliness
and speaks falsely about the LORD;
he leaves the hungry empty
and deprives the thirsty of drink.
7 The weapons of the scoundrel are destructive;
he hatches plots
to destroy the poor with lies,
even when the plea of the needy is just.
8 But a noble man makes honorable plans;
he stands up for worthy causes.

Isaiah 32

If the life that you have lived to this point is, in fact, the best life that you can manage, perhaps you would be well-served to refrain from procreation. Is the world not sufficiently peopled with weaklings, hypocrites, liars, and other human detritus? Dispense with sentimentality for a moment, and give your species an honest assessment. Do not leave *yourself* out of the analysis. Sentimentality about oneself and one's *own* character is tempting, but not excusable. How often has an encounter with your fellow human beings inspired genuine pride and optimism? How long since the last such encounter? You were *not* looking into a mirror, were you? The person staring back at you in that "looking glass" is no paragon of virtue or prowess—and you *know* it. Those folks you encounter outside of your mirror, they have mirrors of their own, do they not? Either what they see is much the same as what you see, or... the drinks ought to be on *you*. It is better for you to be drunk and useless than it is to wander soberly through one day after another, and with a clear head unmitigated by drink, still manage to accomplish nothing of value. Get to work, or get to the saloon. Time is, so far, wasting.

10Then say to them, "This is what the LORD of Hosts, the God
of Israel, says: I will send for My servant Nebuchadnezzar
king of Babylon, and I will set his throne over these stones
that I have embedded, and he will spread his royal pavilion
over them. 11He will come and strike down the land of Egypt,
bringing death to those destined for death, captivity to those
destined for captivity, and the sword to those destined for
the sword.

12I will kindle a fire in the temples of the gods of Egypt, and
he will burn those temples and take their gods as captives.
So he will wrap himself with the land of Egypt as a shepherd
wraps himself in his garment, and he will depart from there
unscathed.

13He will demolish the sacred pillars of the temple of the sun
in Egypt, and he will burn down the temples of the gods of
Egypt."

Jeremiah 43

Are you prepared to endure *anything* that the world might throw your way? Are you prepared to endure frustration, failure, and the inevitable death of your loved ones, as well as your own end? If not, you may as well start digging your own grave. The world *will* have its way with you, precisely as the world will have its way with, and *has* had its way with *every* human being before, during, and after your lifetime. If *any* circumstance is sufficient to "unhorse" you, or enough to make you curl up into the fetal position, then go ahead and assume the position now, because the world *is* going to smash your body, mind, and soul with illness, injury, tragic loss, disappointment, obstruction, and your life will culminate in death, as yours is the same type of human life that destroyed Alexander, Caesar, Newton, Shakespeare,

Einstein, and George Carlin. All of them are *dead*. You *will* follow them to their final destination. Never allow yourself to lose sight of the fact that you are merely another mortal. Will you move forward with courage and a full heart nonetheless, or will you cringe, cower, and shame yourself with irrational terror at the inevitable? Do not delude yourself about the nature of the human condition. You are born to die. Now… *live*!

5 The LORD is gracious and righteous;
our God is full of compassion.
6 The LORD preserves the simplehearted;
I was helpless, and He saved me.
7 Return to your rest, O my soul,
for the LORD has been good to you.
8 For You have delivered my soul from death,
my eyes from tears, my feet from stumbling.

9 I will walk before the LORD
in the land of the living.
10 I believed, therefore I have spoken:
"I am greatly afflicted."
11 In my alarm I said,
"All men are liars!"

Psalm 116

Imbeciles and liars make useless interlocutors. The former lack the capacity to pursue truth or wisdom, whereas the latter have no interest in honest pursuits at all. Conversation, or other forms of exchange, with members of either group is a waste of time, at best, or a perverse submission to some corrupt element of your *own* character. The next time you encounter an assertion that simply cannot be explained by anything other than intellectual deficiency or duplicitous dissembling, simply extricate yourself from the debate or dialogue in question. Just walk away from the exchange. Offer no explanation for doing so. An explanation presented to a moron is a waste of time, effort, and energy. This will only result in further idiocy or prevarication in reply. Try to avoid contributing to the mountain of stupidity already present on the planet. Offer no excuse for withdrawing from the conversation in question. Offer no polite apologies for doing so either. Simply walk away in silence. If the exchange is occurring via some electronic device or online platform, simply desist in offering input. Get your fingers off of the keyboard. Be done with all such nonsense once and for all. Perhaps the liars will entertain the imbeciles.

11 This is what the Lord GOD says: Clap your hands, stomp
your feet, and cry "Alas" for all the wicked abominations
of the house of Israel, who will fall by sword, famine, and
plague. 12 He who is far off will die by the plague, he who is
near will fall by the sword, and he who remains will die of
famine. So I will vent My fury upon them.

13 Then you will know that I am the LORD, when their slain
lie among their idols around their altars, on every high hill,
on all the mountaintops, and under every green tree and
leafy oak—the places where they offered fragrant incense
to all their idols. 14 I will stretch out My hand against them,
and wherever they live I will make the land a desolate waste,
from the wilderness to Diblah. Then they will know that I am
the LORD.

Ezekiel 6

Spoiler Alert: You die at the end of your life! You also have no idea when the end of your life shall come. This is an empirically verifiable fact worth noticing. No claim about life *after* death follows. Perhaps there is a postmortem persistence of the unique, first person perspective that is constitutive of what many think of as the *self*. Perhaps some form of physical resurrection occurs, and embodied selfhood continues, or is re-instigated after the expiration of one's body. Various forms of reincarnation or transmigration of consciousness may be worthy of consideration. Other possibilities present themselves. Then again, it may be that your bodily death is the end of you. Perhaps the termination of electrochemical activity in the brain is the permanent *extinction* of the self. Perhaps your death is the irrecoverable *cessation* of your existence on this planet or anywhere else. You do not know how death "works," and there is no reason to believe that you ever will. Do not pretend to have access to greater or more compelling evidence than is actually available. The body that you think of as "yours" is not long for *this* world. Do not lose sight of this fact. *Memento Mori.* Now, absorb the inevitability of death, and use it to turn your life into something genuinely worth living.

1But understand this: In the last days terrible times will
come. 2For men will be lovers of themselves, lovers of money,
boastful, arrogant, abusive, disobedient to their parents,
ungrateful, unholy, 3unloving, unforgiving, slanderous,
without self-control, brutal, without love of good, 4traitorous,
reckless, conceited, lovers of pleasure rather than lovers of
God, 5having a form of godliness but denying its power. Turn
away from such as these!

2 Timothy 3

Self-loathing is actually a form of narcissism, is it not? How self-absorbed must you be, how obsessed with analysis of yourself, how overawed with contemplation of *you* and that which pertains to *you*, must you be in order to hate yourself with a persisting inward gaze? Thoughts of the self must pervade far too many moments of your internal experience than can possibly be warranted. This is every bit as narcissistic as is excessive love of self, or an overweening desire to aggrandize the fascinating phenomenon that is *you*. What is so captivating about *you*, after all? What justifies any more than the stray, passing notice required to keep yourself alive so that you may get about the real work? Eat food, dodge oncoming vehicles, etc., and then direct your attention to something, some concept, or some project more worthy of attention than *you*. Nearly any other object of attention should suffice. Some are nobler than others, but nearly *all* are more worthy of your time and energy than you. Pay attention where attention is worth the payment.

27 But if a wicked man turns from the wickedness he has
committed and does what is just and right, he will save
his life. 28 Because he considered and turned from all the
transgressions he had committed, he will surely live; he will
not die.

29 Yet the house of Israel says, "The way of the Lord is not
just."

Are My ways unjust, O house of Israel? Is it not your ways that are unjust?

30 Therefore, O house of Israel, I will judge you, each according
to his ways, declares the Lord GOD. Repent and turn from
all your transgressions, so that your iniquity will not become
your downfall.

Ezekiel 18

Someone has been unkind to you without provocation or, at least, without any just cause that you could identify. What of it? You are assured of no particular type of treatment by other persons. You have no right to be treated gently by your fellow talking primates. There is no promise of conviviality and, even if there were, you have long been aware that such promises can be broken upon anyone's whim. Did you expect to be treated, at all times, in all places, and by everyone whom you encounter, in a manner that you find agreeable? What could possibly ground such a ludicrous and obviously counterfactual expectation? Surely, you have sufficient experience to have left such childish assumptions far behind you. The person who mistreated you without justification is the one who is now abased by that misconduct. Why degrade yourself by responding in the same kind of undignified fashion? Do not join the malefactor in irrationality. If you cannot help yourself, then you are no better than is your "tormentor," and you deserve the suffering that you now experience, and that, if you pay attention, you should realize that you impose upon yourself. Surely, you have learned by now that no one can insult you without your complicity. Do not play along. The problem is thereby solved.

19 Remember my affliction and wandering,
the wormwood and the gall.
20 Surely my soul remembers
and is humbled within me.
21 Yet I call this to mind,
and therefore I have hope:

22 Because of the LORD's loving devotion we are not consumed,
for His compassions never fail.
23 They are new every morning;
great is Your faithfulness!
24 "The LORD is my portion," says my soul,
"therefore I will hope in Him."

Lamentations 3

Do not allow your internal life to atrophy due to excessive attention directed outward at conditions that lie beyond your control. Do not neglect that which is genuinely *yours* in a perverse deference to that which has been left to others—or to no one. The world will have its way with external affairs and, indeed, the world will have its way with *you*. The world will, in due time, *kill* you. Keep reminding yourself about the way of all flesh. There lies your future. What of it? Do not obsess about the world "out there." Focus on those phenomena you encounter in the confines of your own consciousness, and those conditions that can be determined by the exertion of *your* will, without the complicity or mediation of other persons, mechanisms, environmental conditions, or anything that is subject to economic or environmental pressures. Your mind is the only domain in which your will holds unmitigated sway. Why hurl your attention into a world that cares nothing for you? Simply reciprocate. Jettison concern for external affairs. Life is on the *inside*. Leave the world to its own devices. It never asked for your help, did it?

11 Now the sea was growing worse and worse, so they said to Jonah, "What must we do to you to calm this sea for us?"

12 "Pick me up," he answered, "and cast me into the sea, so it may quiet down for you. For I know that I am to blame for this violent storm that has come upon you."

13 Nevertheless, the men rowed hard to get back to dry land, but they could not, for the sea was raging against them more and more.

Jonah 1

Solitude is not to be undervalued. Among other persons, you are, at least to some extent, deformed by the presence of observers, and nagging concern about their judgment. Of course, it *should* not be so. Ideally, your character and behavioral tendencies should not be altered by external circumstances, but you are *far* from ideal, are you not? Until you become a sage (and do not hold your breath awaiting this development), it will be necessary to withdraw, periodically, to a place apart from others, separated from prying eyes, and free from enervating interactions that sap your energy and impede your progress toward wisdom and virtue. Find a place of your own. Let mind and body rest and replenish their vital energies. Find an area of relatively easily established serenity, and readily maintained equanimity. Let this place function as a doorway to the *inner* citadel of your unconquerable mind. Keep the inside tidy, calm, and private. Do not allow other persons to rummage through the contents of your consciousness. Doing so invites contamination.

10 Yet it was the LORD's will to crush Him and cause Him to suffer.
And when His soul is made a guilt offering,
He will see His offspring, He will prolong His days,
and the good pleasure of the LORD will prosper in His hand.
11 After the anguish of His soul,
He will see the light of life and be satisfied.
By His knowledge My righteous Servant will justify many,
and He will bear their iniquities.
12 Therefore I will allot Him a portion with the great,
and He will divide the spoils with the strong,
because He has poured out His life unto death,
and He was numbered among the transgressors.
Yet He bore the sin of many
and made intercession for the transgressors.

Isaiah 53

Crush the weakness and vice within you. Extirpate those inclinations as thoroughly as you are able. Do not accept the opinion of the masses about what does or does not constitute vice and virtue. The general public is a stunningly unreliable moral barometer. Indeed, there often seems to be something of an inverted or upside-down and inside-out moral compass guiding the misguided public at large. Weakness is all-too-often held up as a virtue, and the useless hoi polloi frequently embrace the most repulsive vice. In any event, do not conflate the common conception of "virtue" with virtue *itself*. Your compass is to be attuned to the wisdom of the ages, rather than the received opinion of any single moment in time, or any particular segment of this or that culture. Look to Sinai. Look to Athens. Find those themes that are common to both, and that undergird Western civilization. Look to that without which decency would have died. Do not ignore the East, or other legitimate wellsprings of wisdom, but seek the bedrock of the cultural soil from which you have grown. There are reliable guides to be found in the ancient texts, and in the recorded words of the sages. By the way, what are *you* doing to keep the pursuit of wisdom and decency alive?

4 My heart murmurs within me,
and the terrors of death assail me.
5 Fear and trembling grip me,
and horror has overwhelmed me.
6 I said, "Oh, that I had wings like a dove!
I would fly away and find rest.
7 How far away I would flee;
in the wilderness I would remain."

Psalm 55

You are beset by uncertainty again today, are you not? Perhaps there is a legitimate reason to be uncertain about the course this day shall take, or about your conduct in response to those challenges that may arise today. What, however, is the justification for being emotionally "beset" by impending possibilities. What, exactly, is the benefit of worrying and obsessively contemplating unpleasant contingencies that may or may not occur and, more importantly, conditions that actually lie within *your* power, and are subject to the proper management of your desire, aversion, reason, and action? Your fears are, ultimately, manifestations of self-doubt and insecurities about the potential weakness of your will. The world will unfold as forces beyond your control cause it to unfold. This *cannot* be any concern to a rational agent. Only irrationality can result in concern about matters beyond your control. No, you fear that you will not prove adequate to the challenge of this day. Do not fear. The fear in and of itself will do you no good. Prepare. Steel yourself. When the challenges arise, act in accordance with reason. That is the most you can do.

14For this is what the LORD of Hosts says: "Just as I resolved
to bring disaster upon you when your fathers provoked Me
to anger, and I did not relent," says the LORD of Hosts, 15"so
now I have resolved to do good again to Jerusalem and Judah.
Do not be afraid. 16These are the things you must do: Speak
truth to one another, render true and sound decisions in your
gates, 17do not plot evil in your hearts against your neighbor,
and do not love perjury, for I hate all these things," declares
the LORD.

Zechariah 8

Seek the truth wherever the search may take you, or admit that you are more interested in comfort than you are in honesty, decency, or wisdom. If you refuse to acknowledge uncomfortable truths, or if you cling to pleasant falsehoods because of the hedonic benefits of so doing, then lie down, pull up the covers, and watch cartoons until you drop dead. The *truth* is to be, in *all* of your endeavors, the overarching aim and object. "Truth or death" is preferable to "comfort or anxiety," is it not? Were you born to reside in a cloud castle of childish illusion? Look the world in the eye, and understand your true place within it. Let integrity be your guide in all endeavors. Adopt the posture of a stalwart and meet any and all contingencies face to face. Let the world throw what it may in your direction, and do not flinch at any fate. Most have led *far* more difficult lives than you can readily imagine, and you *dare* bemoan the day to come? Weakling! Coward! Gird your loins and enter the arena with your head up and your eyes open. The lions are waiting. Give them a challenge, at least. Otherwise, you are no more than a meal.

29 And God gave Solomon wisdom, exceedingly deep insight,
and understanding beyond measure, like the sand on the
seashore. 30 Solomon's wisdom was greater than that of all
the men of the East, greater than all the wisdom of Egypt.
31 He was wiser than all men—wiser than Ethan the Ezrahite,
and wiser than Heman, Calcol, and Darda, the sons of Mahol.
And his fame spread throughout the surrounding nations.

32 Solomon composed three thousand proverbs, and his songs
numbered a thousand and five. 33 He spoke of trees, from the
cedar in Lebanon to the hyssop growing in the wall, and he
taught about animals, birds, reptiles, and fish.

34 So men of all nations came to listen to Solomon's wisdom,
sent by all the kings of the earth when they heard of his
wisdom.

1 Kings 4

Draw your water from the deepest well you can find. Those who skim the surface will find their meager efforts "rewarded" with meaningless platitudes and bumper sticker "wisdom." Do not content yourself with spouting the occasional witticism or the stray shibboleth. Do not pose as an Oracle in some misguided attempt to impress slack wits and charlatans. They have consigned themselves to the oblivion of mediocrity, ignorance, and commentary upon the shadows dancing on the walls of Plato's cave. They signal to each other and puff themselves up with false shows of virtue. Do not allow yourself to become one of these children desperately seeking approval from one another—as they shudder at an adult's approach. Your job is to be the adult who shatters their illusions and demonstrates a life worthy of emulation. Nourish yourself from the depths of the well that they cannot fathom. Drink the deeps dry if you can.

Perhaps someone else may follow your example. Perhaps you will go unnoticed. This is *nothing* to you.

7Light is sweet,
and it pleases the eyes to see the sun.
8So if a man lives many years,
let him rejoice in them all;
but let him remember the days of darkness,
for they will be many.
Everything to come is futile.

9Rejoice, O young man, while you are young,
and let your heart be glad in the days of your youth.
Walk in the ways of your heart and in the sight of your eyes,
but know that for all these things God will bring you to judgment.
10So banish sorrow from your heart,
and cast off pain from your body,
for youth and vigor are fleeting.

Ecclesiastes 11

Take all of your worries, anxieties, and self-doubts in the palm of one hand. Now, clench your fist and punch yourself in the face, stupid. That would be wiser, healthier, and more productive than all of your incessant internal handwringing, jabbering, and relentless perseveration, would it not? What good does this reflexive rumination upon darkness and potential calamity do you? Tell that whimpering voice of doubt to shut up and get out of your presence once and for all. You know that voice lies. Indeed, that is *all* it ever has done. The liar tells you that you cannot succeed, that you dare not try, that you are an imposter wearing a stolen suit of armor. The liar has been there for as far back as you can remember. The liar whispered to you in your crib. The time to evict the liar is at hand. Indeed, that time has been "at hand" since you were a child. Are you *still* a child? Are you afraid to grow up? Kill the liar. Show no mercy. Drive a stake in—and break it off. No mercy for the voice of this enemy.

15 If anyone attacks you,
it is not from Me;
whoever assails you
will fall before you.
16 Behold, I have created the craftsman
who fans the coals into flame
and forges a weapon
fit for its task;
and I have created the destroyer
to wreak havoc.
17 No weapon formed against you shall prosper,
and you will refute every tongue that accuses you.
This is the heritage of the LORD's servants,
and their vindication is from Me...

Isaiah 54

The suggestion that "we are all created equal" is moronic pabulum that is demonstrably false, and nothing more than a bit of verbal Valium to assuage the anxiety of the masses. It is an opiate or a hypnotist's trick. Never embrace silly platitudes merely because they are commonly expressed or blithely asserted. Do not succumb to this insidious bit of cultural mesmerism. Are you intellectually comparable to Einstein? Do you possess the artistic prowess of Michelangelo? Can you approach the musical attainments of Beethoven? Demonstrate your athletic equality with the greatest Olympians if you can. How ridiculous this presumption of equality proves to be. Are we all "equals in God's eyes"? That claim is both presumptuous and unverifiable. Even if true, the equality inheres in God's "eyes," and not in you or your fellow talking primates. Those who hold equality up as a regulative ideal are no better than herd animals. Perhaps all sheep are equal. Do you wish to be a sheep? If not, put this nonsense behind you. If you seek equality, what does that tell you about your current condition? Alexander the Great did not strive to be "the equal" of his fellow man.

March

8 Then I heard the voice of the Lord saying,

"Whom shall I send?
Who will go for Us?"

And I said,

"Here am I. Send me!"

9 And He replied, "Go and tell this people:

'Be ever hearing, but never understanding;
be ever seeing, but never perceiving.'
10 Make the hearts of this people calloused;
deafen their ears and close their eyes.
Otherwise they might see with their eyes,
hear with their ears,
understand with their hearts,
and turn and be healed."

Isaiah 6

Your will can only be broken from the inside, and only *you* can break it. Do not blame external circumstances for your failures of determination, resolve, or grit. Do not tell yourself that some challenge is too daunting for you to face it head on, courageously, and with a gleam in your eye. To be sure, there are many trials that will prove to be too great for you to conquer, and many conditions in the external world that you cannot surmount, but there is *nothing* and no threat that you cannot
a fearless warrior. There is no shame in getti
an opponent. Some are simply bigger, strong
skilled, etc. It is, however, shameful to allow
intimidated, cowed, or frightened into submis

may break. Indeed, your body *will* break sooner or later. That is not within the power of your will. If your spirit breaks, however, blame no one and nothing other than yourself. Now, prepare for battle. Forward. *Always* forward.

1Then Zophar the Naamathite replied:
2"Should this stream of words go unanswered
and such a speaker be vindicated?
3Should your babbling put others to silence?
Will you scoff without rebuke?
4You have said, 'My doctrine is sound,
and I am pure in Your sight.'
5But if only God would speak
and open His lips against you,
6and disclose to you the secrets of wisdom,
for true wisdom has two sides.
Know then that God exacts from you
less than your iniquity deserves.

7Can you fathom the deep things of God
or discover the limits of the Almighty?
8They are higher than the heavens—what can you do?
They are deeper than Sheol—what can you know?
9Their measure is longer than the earth
and wider than the sea."

Job 11

Sometimes you feel as if you are racking your brain in the attempt to recall the words to a poem that no one ever wrote—but that someone *should* have written. It feels as if the perfect words are just "out of sight" (so to speak), just outside the reach of your memory or imagination. Is this some type of cognitive illusion or dysfunction, or is there, in fact, something hovering just beyond your intellectual horizons, waiting impatiently for your discovery or recollection? Can you have an obligation to an abstraction that may or may not actually exist? Consider a duty attaching to a mere possibility. At first consideration, this seems absurd, but how much scientific progress might have been lost in the absence of this sensed obligation to pursue a something-one-knows-not-what to which a stray intuition has been attracted? Listen to the words of the works as yet unwritten. If necessary, *write* the words that beg to be brought into the light.

1 Deliver me from my enemies, O my God;
protect me from those who rise against me.
2 Deliver me from workers of iniquity,
and save me from men of bloodshed.
3 See how they lie in wait for me.
Fierce men conspire against me
for no transgression or sin of my own, O LORD.
4 For no fault of my own,
they move swiftly to attack me.
Arise to help me, and take notice.
5 O LORD God of Hosts, the God of Israel,
rise up to punish all the nations;
show no mercy to the wicked traitors.
Selah
6 They return in the evening,
snarling like dogs
and prowling around the city.

Psalm 59

Beware the vampires of the spirit, and of the life force. Vampires who suck blood from the carotid artery are, of course, merely the stuff of fiction and phantasmagoria. Metaphorical vampires siphon away your time, your energy, and your attention, and are to be guarded against with far more potent countermeasures than garlic, holy water, and a crucifix. Those who suckle away at your *life* and offer you nothing in return, or even undercut your vital energies apart from the aforementioned resources, must be driven out of your life as if your humanity and your integrity hang in the balance. Such matters *do* hang in the balance, do they not? Allowing yourself to be victimized is *never* a virtue, and *never* ennobles you. Do not allow appeals to "compassion" into your reasoning about this matter. Vampires are not entitled to compassion. They get a stake through the heart. Make sure to burn away the remnants. Salt the earth and saturate the deep grave.

1 And the LORD said to Job:

2 "Will the faultfinder contend with the Almighty?
Let him who argues with God give an answer."

3 Then Job answered the LORD:

4 "Behold, I am insignificant. How can I reply to You?
I place my hand over my mouth.
5 I have spoken once, but I have no answer—
twice, but I have nothing to add."

Job 40

Wake up, get out of bed, get cleaned up, and get to work without whining, whimpering, complaining, or procrastinating before the challenges of this day. Who are *you* to complain about *anything*? If the advantages afforded you are insufficient to forestall your self-pity, then just lie down and die already, you pathetic, useless weakling. How dare you buckle under the incredibly slight burdens that you bear? Consider the common human lot throughout all of recorded history, and recognize what we can safely infer about conditions prior to the earliest records. What percentage of your forebears had it easier than you? Surely, the number is vanishingly small. Look around the world as it stands today. How many have, like you, *never* known hunger? How many have never experienced oppression? How many have never been within one thousand miles of warfare? Share tales of your "challenges" with others if you must. Do *not* expect sympathy from anyone. None is warranted. Gratitude—not griping.

6 Of course, godliness with contentment is great gain. 7 For
we brought nothing into the world, and neither can we carry
anything out of it. 8 But if we have food and clothing, we will
be content with these.

9 Those who want to be rich, however, fall into temptation
and become ensnared by many foolish and harmful desires
that plunge them into ruin and destruction. 10 For the love of
money is the root of all kinds of evil. By craving it, some have
wandered away from the faith and pierced themselves with
many sorrows.

1 Timothy 6

There is no shame in starting with the smaller challenges, and gradually building up your resistance to temptation, as well as slowly expanding your sphere of self-mastery. Begin by choosing to attempt reasonably tractable tasks and endeavors. Work your way up to a full-scale value system, a worldview, and the proper governance of your overarching life goals. Begin, for example, by walking rather than using your car or some other mechanized conveyance. Note that the walking does you no harm. Indeed, you are likely to find that is quite healthy for you, both physiologically and emotionally. More than one particularly fecund idea manifested while the thinker took a walk. Begin by eating vegetables rather than sweets or other foods that do your body little good, and serve only as mindless satisfaction of a desire, not a need, and one that can be laid aside fairly readily and with significant benefit. Identify an unwise or unwholesome habit of speech, and substitute a more palatable, thoughtful alternative. These are the building blocks upon which your citadel shall stand. Lay the foundation. Begin at the beginning.

1 And God spoke all these words:

2 "I am the LORD your God, who brought you out of the land
of Egypt, out of the house of slavery.

3 You shall have no other gods before Me.

4 You shall not make for yourself an idol of any kind, or an
image of anything in the heavens above, on the earth beneath,
or in the waters below. 5 You shall not bow down to them
or worship them; for I, the LORD your God, am a jealous
God, visiting the iniquity of the fathers on their children to
the third and fourth generations of those who hate Me, 6 but
showing loving devotion to a thousand generations of those
who love Me and keep My commandments."

Exodus 20

The Second Commandment is an injunction to eschew the worship of anything other than God, and a warning about the consequences, for your own character and for those with whom you come into contact, of elevating that which is not holy to a status that is properly reserved *only* for the Creator. Belief in God is not necessary to perceive the wisdom in this counsel. Simply observe the wake of destruction trailing those who allow themselves to worship power, money, fame, nation, race, false prophets, or other elements of the imperfect and impure world. The ruins lie about you everywhere, and they litter history as well. If there is no God to worship, then withhold this elevated reverence entirely. *Worship* has no proper object other than the Almighty. Are you not better off living *as if* God is watching as opposed to the alternative absence of transcendent purpose? The question is sincere and worthy of careful consideration. If there exists no ultimate arbiter of justice, or of good and evil, you would still do well to pursue justice and virtue, and to avoid evil. If there is some reward for so doing, all the better.

18 Caravans turn aside from their routes;
they go into the wasteland and perish.
19 The caravans of Tema look for water;
the travelers of Sheba hope to find it.
20 They are confounded by their confidence;
their arrival brings disappointment.
21 For now you are of no help;
you see terror, and you are afraid.
22 Have I ever said: "Give me something;
offer me a bribe from your wealth;
23 deliver me from the hand of the enemy;
redeem me from the grasp of the ruthless"?

Job 6

Has some miscreant or charlatan attempted to take advantage of you? Was the attempt successful? Well, *whose* fault is that, and what is to be said of it? If you blame the malefactor, you ignore the influence of heredity and environment upon character formation, habit, and subsequent behavior. Would you insist that anyone "must be otherwise," or would you insist that the world and its inhabitants are deficient because your desires are not always satisfied or your aversions are sometimes incurred? The world, then, disappoints you? So, hold the world accountable if you can. Cast aspersions wherever you please. What good would any of that do you, and do you not feel absurd for castigating reality as it stands? Only a petulant child renders judgment against the world. Such foolishness! Learn to guard against mistreatment, or learn to retain your equanimity in spite of it (or both), but recognize that *you* and your poorly disciplined mind are the cause of your dissatisfaction. Do not *allow* people to take advantage of you. Get ahold of yourself. Release your grip on the world.

17 The righteous cry out, and the LORD hears;
He delivers them from all their troubles.
18 The LORD is near to the brokenhearted;
He saves the contrite in spirit.

19 Many are the afflictions of the righteous,
but the LORD delivers him from them all.
20 He protects all his bones;
not one of them will be broken.

21 Evil will slay the wicked,
and the haters of the righteous will be condemned.
22 The LORD redeems His servants,
and none who take refuge in Him will be condemned.

Psalm 34

Everyone is flawed. This is not a particularly controversial claim. Only lunatics or liars deny anything so patently obvious as this. It is, of course, equally clear that some are flawed far more acutely, intensely, pervasively, and in a manner with much more serious consequences than are others. Stalin is far worse than is a sneak thief who purloins a pack of cigarettes. You are not permitted to hide behind your own imperfections as a method of avoiding the burdens associated with passing public judgment upon the most pernicious malefactors of your day and age. You are not to be silenced by the chastisement that "nobody is perfect." Meet that charge with the candid admission that you are as bad as just about anyone else, and that you are worse than many (perhaps even most persons)—but terrorists, genocidal maniacs, and those who sexually assault children are not properly regarded as *persons* at all. These are not merely "imperfect" persons. These are monsters. It may not, in the final analysis, be their fault that they are monsters, but their culpability, or lack thereof, does not alter the necessity of standing athwart their purposes. Do what needs to be done. Let them dangle from a short rope. Sometimes *mercy* is a sin.

137 Righteous are You, O LORD,
and upright are Your judgments.
138 The testimonies You have laid down are righteous
and altogether faithful.
139 My zeal has consumed me
because my foes forget Your words.
140 Your promise is completely pure;
therefore Your servant loves it.
141 I am lowly and despised,
but I do not forget Your precepts.
142 Your righteousness is an everlasting righteousness,
and Your law is true.
143 Trouble and distress have found me,
but Your commandments are my delight.
144 Your testimonies are righteous forever.
Give me understanding, that I may live.

Psalm 119

Who are these persons that arrogate, to their own devices, the right to compel you to care about issues that have, in fact, no purchase upon your concern or your interests? Evidently, there exist those individuals and groups who believe that they are entitled to determine that you will be *made to care* about their pet issues, concerns, and idiosyncratic causes. You are both a fool and a weakling if you spend even one full second considering the motives or interests of the pathetic cultural cry-bullies. Who are these people that you should pay them anything more than *no mind* whatsoever? Let them cry. Let them whine. Let them accuse you of absolutely anything and everything they may conjure and impute to you. What is *any* of that adolescent nonsense to you? These are sheep bleating in unison. Embrace their accusations. Confess that you are even worse than they imagine. Admit, publicly, that you simply *do not care* about those issues concerning which they accuse you, quite correctly, of indifference. Simply tell the truth. Focus on legitimate concerns that are worthy of your attention. Admit that all the rest is *nothing* to you. Nothing. Let the herd animals trudge along together in their phony bovine self-righteousness. They do not even warrant a smirk.

7 These also stagger from wine
and stumble from strong drink:
Priests and prophets reel from strong drink
and are befuddled by wine.
They stumble because of strong drink,
muddled in their visions and stumbling in their judgments.
8 For all their tables are covered with vomit;
there is not a place without filth.

9 Who is it He is trying to teach?
To whom is He explaining His message?
To infants just weaned from milk?
To babies removed from the breast?

Isaiah 28

Gaze upon everything that you do not want, and every person with whom you wish to have *nothing* to do. Those elements of the world that are worthy of your notice, and useful to your self-improvement, are shockingly scarce. The useless, the detritus, the ignoble, and the unworthy, they lie before you and around you everywhere. The garbage is spread around the globe, hurled seemingly everywhere, in the ubiquitous sludge of mediocrity and filth that masquerades as someone's "culture." What is this disaster area that you once thought of as "your" home? If *this* is home, and if *this* is yours—walk away from home, and find a quiet place in the wilderness. It is better that you live your life in isolation than that you partake in the disgusting charade that unfolds relentlessly across all media and, somewhat disturbingly, across the minds of your "fellow citizens." You are free to walk away from *all* of it. Your life is *yours* to govern. You never pledged allegiance to stupidity, you never swore to uphold and defend indecency, and you never gave your word that you would fight to the death in defense of pathologies and injustice. Your life's purpose has absolutely nothing to do with the denizens of these ghost towns that masquerade as "your" society. Look for the signposts to decency and honor. A worthwhile journey lies before you. Get to it.

1 Hear the word of the LORD,
O children of Israel,
for the LORD has a case
against the inhabitants of the land:
There is no truth, no loving devotion,
and no knowledge of God in the land!
2 Cursing and lying,
murder and stealing,
and adultery are rampant;
one act of bloodshed follows another.
3 Therefore the land mourns,
and all who dwell in it will waste away
with the beasts of the field and the birds of the air;
even the fish of the sea disappear.

Hosea 4

Do not take anything that is not given to you freely, purchased honestly, or bartered in good faith. This rule pertains not only to material goods, but also to intellectual property, persons, and reputations. Never build your legacy upon the backs of those who do not consent to be part of your narrative. Persons who do not wish to be mentioned may have good reason for this preference, as they may decline involvement due to fear, indifference, or, perhaps, even petulance. This is no business of yours. Their reason need not "satisfy" you. You have no authority to demand an explanation that satisfies your sensibilities. No one is obligated to be any part of your "story," or of the message you intend to share, or to have anything else to do with you at all. How many times have you found yourself drawn into plans or schemes that you would have avoided had you been offered fair warning of the intentions and probable outcome in question? What exactly *is* this business of "using" other persons without their consent or, worse still, contrarily to their wishes? Persons are *not* your playthings. Humanity is no mere tool. Without their consent, you are entitled to nothing from persons other than yourself.

1 He who isolates himself pursues selfish desires;
he rebels against all sound judgment.

2 A fool does not delight in understanding,
but only in airing his opinions.

3 With a wicked man comes contempt as well,
and shame is accompanied by disgrace.

4 The words of a man's mouth are deep waters;
the fountain of wisdom is a bubbling brook.

Proverbs 18

Be prepared, at a moment's notice, to walk away from any endeavor you find to be ignoble or dishonest, and any person or group that you find to be less than wholesome and scrupulous. Do not tether yourself to anyone or anything that is not worthy of your limited time and energy. Lives are often wasted in pursuit of money, fame, or power. Worse yet, lives are sometimes spent in self-abasement pursuing goals that serve only the dark and contemptible elements of human nature and the behaviors to which it is susceptible. It is better to live and die as an unknown pauper than it is to attain vaunted heights of power and influence at the expense of your decency. Only your character, your "soul" (if you will) travels with you as far as you may go. Money stays with your corpse until human vultures carry it away. Fame remains here only if you are remembered. You will not be remembered for long. Even if you were to be remembered for as long as the human race lasts, it should be fairly clear that the human race will not last forever, and being remembered by your fellow talking apes is no great achievement in any event. Political power is powerless to forestall mortality. Both individually and collectively, "we" are all destined for extinction. People only last so long. Compared to the oceans of time and space, we are trifling creatures. Govern your *soul*—mortal or immortal. It *is* your humanity.

5 David and all the house of Israel were celebrating before the
LORD with all kinds of wood instruments, harps, stringed
instruments, tambourines, sistrums, and cymbals.

6 When they came to the threshing floor of Nachon, Uzzah
reached out and took hold of the ark of God, because the
oxen had stumbled. 7 And the anger of the LORD burned
against Uzzah, and God struck him down on the spot for his
irreverence, and he died there beside the ark of God.

8 Then David became angry because the LORD had burst forth
against Uzzah; so he named that place Perez-uzzah, as it is
called to this day.

2 Samuel 6

Your failures are *yours* alone, and any attempt to blame them on someone or something else is cowardly self-abasement. Do you hold the world at large accountable for your behavior? Do you *blame* the world? If so, admit that you are no better than an automaton, or a programmed computer, and relinquish any and all claims to personhood or moral significance. If you are, in fact, no more than the world has made you, then stop your arrogant, prideful boasting at every success—just as you childishly demand to be absolved of every failure and defeat, so too you can claim no credit for any triumph. Events unfold, and forces beyond your control cause them to be as they are. If, on the other hand, you are not a mere product of heredity and environment, if you are not a chance concatenation of circumstances beyond your control, then embrace *all* that you make of yourself. Take full responsibility for *everything* about your character, your behavior, and the consequences thereof. If you insist upon puffing yourself up when you succeed, do not point fingers elsewhere when you fail. You cannot, with a straight face, cherry-pick the events that constitute your life, and only take ownership of those events that you find "convenient" for portraying, to the rest of the world, a persona that barely resembles you. Your life is *all* or *nothing*. Take responsibility for all of it.

28"The rest of the people—the priests, Levites, gatekeepers,
singers, and temple servants, and all who had separated
themselves from the people of the land to obey the law of
God—along with their wives and all their sons and daughters
who were able to understand, 29hereby join with their noble
brothers and commit themselves with a sworn oath to follow
the Law of God given through His servant Moses and to
carefully obey all the commandments, ordinances, and
statutes of the LORD our Lord.

30We will not give our daughters in marriage to the people of
the land, and we will not take their daughters for our sons."

Nehemiah 10

Never indulge in casuistry. It is always disingenuous, cowardly, and ignoble. Do not decide, on a particular occasion, what the moral facts simply *must* be, and then massage the evidence to rationalize your pre-reflective view of the matter at hand. Moral laws must be objective, universal, and invariant—or they are neither moral nor *laws* at all. Changing rules are all well and good for civil constructs (drive on the right side of the road in the States, and on the left in England), but evil, if it exists at all, must remain what it is, even if it is divorced from time, place, culture, and all the rest. If raping a child is evil (and if it is *not*, God help us all), then it must be so no matter who does it, where it occurs, when it happens, or whatever the consequences may be. If doing *that* is required for saving the world, then let the world perish. Moral cowardice produces moral relativism, and you are not permitted to degrade yourself by indulging in this form of intellectual dishonesty. Moral relativism is just nihilism dressed up in fancy clothes. Moral facts are objective and absolute—or they are *nothing*.

20 He who walks with the wise will become wise,
but the companion of fools will be destroyed.

21 Disaster pursues sinners,
but prosperity is the reward of the righteous.

22 A good man leaves an inheritance to his children's children,
but the sinner's wealth is passed to the righteous.

23 Abundant food is in the fallow ground of the poor,
but without justice it is swept away.

24 He who spares the rod hates his son,
but he who loves him disciplines him diligently.

25 A righteous man eats to his heart's content,
but the stomach of the wicked is empty.

Proverbs 13

Injustice has been a fact of the human condition for, probably, about as long as there have been humans. No evidence suggests that injustice will disappear within your lifetime or, indeed, at any time—so long as human beings exist. To bemoan this fact is pointlessly childish. To stamp your feet and insist that the world *must* be other than it is, or that human nature *must* be altered in some manner that has never occurred, is to succumb to sullen irrationality. If you wish to be both petulant and irrational, if you wish to whine and moan about ineradicable conditions, then please note the exits staring you in the face everywhere. If you are too pathetic and weak to face the world as it stands, and to live your life as it unfolds, then shut up and dive off of a mountain, step in front of a train, or take a sharp object to your carotid artery. You whimper about injustice? Does the whimpering help to eradicate the injustice? Find your justice in death, if you are too emotionally fragile for this life.

April

1 Behold, my eyes have seen all this;
my ears have heard and understood.
2 What you know, I also know;
I am not inferior to you.
3 Yet I desire to speak to the Almighty
and argue my case before God.
4 You, however, smear with lies;
you are all worthless physicians.
5 If only you would be silent;
for that would be your wisdom!

6 Hear now my argument,
and listen to the plea of my lips.
7 Will you speak wickedly on God's behalf
or speak deceitfully for Him?
8 Would you show Him partiality
or argue in His defense?
9 Would it be well when He examined you?
Could you deceive Him like a man?
10 Surely He would rebuke you
if you secretly showed partiality.
11 Would His majesty not terrify you?
Would the dread of Him not fall upon you?
12 Your maxims are proverbs of ashes;
your defenses are defenses of clay.

Job 13

You will probably never talk anyone out of their most cherished beliefs or most closely-held values. Never allow your peace of mind to depend upon getting anyone else to agree with you. Opinions change if sufficient experience *causes* a change, and if the "true believer" is sufficiently honest and introspective to allow the relevant experience to take hold. Make your best effort to present the most compelling available argumentation and evidence, explain it all with the greatest perspicacity you can muster, and then relinquish any emotional attachment to your argument taking root, or leading to any alteration in your interlocutor's perspective. Do not insist upon successfully reaching into any "hearts and minds" apart from your own. Is there insufficient detritus to clear away from your own all-too-hazy worldview? See to your own cleansing and rectification. Be an example—not a pest. No one enjoys keeping company with a hectoring scold.

32 David said to Saul, "Let no man's heart fail on account of this Philistine. Your servant will go and fight him!"

33 But Saul replied, "You cannot go out against this Philistine to fight him. You are just a boy, and he has been a warrior from his youth."

34 David replied, "Your servant has been tending his father's
sheep, and whenever a lion or a bear came and carried off
a lamb from the flock, 35 I went after it, struck it down, and
delivered the lamb from its mouth. If it reared up against
me, I would grab it by its fur, strike it down, and kill it.
36 Your servant has killed lions and bears; this uncircumcised
Philistine will be like one of them, for he has defied the armies
of the living God."

37 David added, "The LORD who delivered me from the claws of the lion and the bear will deliver me from the hand of this Philistine."

"Go," said Saul, "and may the LORD be with you."

1 Samuel 17

David slew Goliath, but that was not his moment of triumph. The greater victory was won at the moment he decided to face the seemingly invincible foe in the name of his God, his people, and in the name of virtue. David overcame his fear, and he was able to call upon his fortitude, gather his courage, and compel himself to sally forth into battle, because he believed that his cause was just and his valor, indeed, even his sacrifice, might have been necessary in the pursuit of justice, honor, and a greater good. Are you confident that you will behave in like fashion should the opportunity arise? If not, you had better begin hardening your spine and bolstering your strength of character. Should you be called upon to risk all that you possess in the name of something greater than yourself or your narrow interests, you are obligated to answer that call—even if you know that answering will be the end of you. Better to die in virtue, than to persist in vice, shame, and ignominy. Live in honor, or die in disgrace.

1 This is the oracle of Nineveh, the book of the vision of Nahum
the Elkoshite:

2 The LORD is a jealous and avenging God;
the LORD is avenging and full of wrath.
The LORD takes vengeance on His foes
and reserves wrath for His enemies.
3 The LORD is slow to anger
and great in power;
the LORD will by no means
leave the guilty unpunished.
His path is in the whirlwind and storm,
and clouds are the dust beneath His feet.
4 He rebukes the sea and dries it up;
He makes all the rivers run dry.
Bashan and Carmel wither,
and the flower of Lebanon wilts.

Nahum 1

You can see that a storm is on its way, and you can feel a very long winter following in the wake of that storm. Do not mourn those who are about to perish because they insist upon denying the thunderclouds all across the horizon. They are entitled to their comforting delusions and their cloud castles of imaginary peace, prosperity, and stability. They are not, however, entitled to have the rest of us take their delusions seriously, or to bend governments, corporations, and other "powers that be" to indulge them, or to behave in accordance with the dictates of their misapprehensions. Little purpose is served by sounding alarms that the masses are bent on ignoring. The public is an unruly beast, and not yours to control. *You* are not, thereby, absolved of responsibility for making the necessary preparations merely because others fail to perceive the necessity. The weak, the stupid, and the credulous will suffer what they must. Sloth and idiocy have always incurred unfortunate consequences, and both have proven immune to all attempted cures. When the storm comes, do not risk your loved ones in an attempt to save those who are unworthy of salvation. Let the sleepwalkers perish. Do not turn back when you hear them screaming.

8 Very soon I will pour out My wrath upon you
and vent My anger against you;
I will judge you according to your ways
and punish you for all your abominations.
9 I will not look on you with pity,
nor will I spare you,
but I will punish you for your ways
and for the abominations among you.
Then you will know that it is I, the LORD,
who strikes the blow.

10 Behold, the day is here!
It has come!
Doom has gone out,
the rod has budded,
arrogance has bloomed.
11 Their violence has grown into a rod
to punish their wickedness.
None of them will remain:
none of their multitude,
none of their wealth,
and nothing of value.

Ezekiel 7

Do not stretch out your desires toward objects that are not subject to the control of your will and tethered to determination by your choices. If you cannot will a condition into being, withdraw your desire from that condition, and do not allow your contentment to rest upon external states of affairs coming to fruition. The world "out there" unfolds, evolves, and flows along in accordance with forces that are entirely outside your sphere of influence. Do not, therefore, insist that the external world *must* be thus-and-so, or you shall respond to events with despair and childish pugnacity.

The world is to be "taken as it comes," or it is to be rejected in irrational petulance. Do you believe that the world is *obligated* to satisfy your desires? This is absurd. This is idiocy. This is narcissism not befitting an allegedly rational agent. Find *your* way. Do not insist that a path must be cleared for you. Blaze new trails where you can and must, and avoid those well-trodden paths that lead to damnation.

4 "I will stretch out My hand against Judah
and against all who dwell in Jerusalem.
I will cut off from this place
every remnant of Baal,
the names of the idolatrous
and pagan priests—
5 those who bow on the rooftops
to worship the heavenly host,
those who bow down and swear by the LORD
but also swear by Molech,
6 and those who turn back
from following the LORD
and neither seek the LORD
nor inquire of Him."

Zephaniah 1

What do you care for the competitions of the day, or the pointless adversarial spectacles of sports, politics, and international intrigue? The outcome is of no more than academic interest in most cases—and not even *that* in many instances. One nation takes advantage of another in trade relations. *All* trade deals involve winners and losers, predators and prey. Not one has ever been equitable, nor have any been intended to be equitable. What is this to you, and what are you supposed to do about it? One of the nations involved is "yours," is it? In what sense is *any* nation *yours*? You did not construct or conceive it. You do not sustain it, and "your" nation would take no notice of your death or your departure. You live in it. Perhaps you were born in it. You pay taxes to its governing bodies. Its name appears on your passport. That is all—and all of that is, more or less, nothing. Be prepared to shed concern with "your" nation and walk away if that nation ceases to be worthy of your allegiance, or if you realize that it never was worthy in the first place. Still more, be prepared to cast off any concerns attaching to political parties, or collectives that are grounded in anything other than familial connections. Do not chain yourself to a squalid abstraction. As for sports teams—grow up already. Games are best left to children. Are *you* a child?

13 The godless in heart harbor resentment;
even when He binds them, they do not cry for help.
14 They die in their youth;
and their life ends among the male cult prostitutes.
15 God rescues the afflicted by their affliction
and opens their ears in oppression.

Job 36

Suffering that cannot be avoided must be endured and you must embrace your life complete with "warts and all." Imagined alternatives only exacerbate and intensify the psychological and emotional distress needlessly. You must understand that some forms of suffering cannot be dispelled, and your embrace of life in those conditions must *not* be disingenuous. *Pretending* to make friends with your suffering, and the attendant repression of your dissatisfaction will only generate some form of neurosis, or an abiding resentment that will eat away at your intestines as well as your serenity. The injury that never quite healed, that proves resistant to all palliative measures, and produces relentless discontent and disability *must* be treated as if it is woven into the deepest fibers of your being, and as if it *belongs* with you as does any other ineradicable facet of your physical makeup. An incurable illness or injury ought to be regarded in much the same way that you regard physical characteristics that are determined by your genetic endowment. It is to be treated as part and parcel of your unique, individual experience of the human condition. It is foolish to treat your suffering as if it is an injustice, as if it is an oppressive cross that you deserve not to bear, or as if it is some form of punishment imposed upon you by a malevolent despot bent on ruining your life. Your suffering is closer to you than is the iris of your eye. Proceed accordingly. Carry your burdens, and do not complain about them—not even in the confines of your own mind.

1 You shall not spread a false report. Do not join the wicked by
being a malicious witness.

2 You shall not follow a crowd in wrongdoing. When you
testify in a lawsuit, do not pervert justice by siding with a
crowd. 3 And do not show favoritism to a poor man in his
lawsuit.

Exodus 23

All collectivism is expressible as the weakness, timidity, and cowardice of individuals writ large. The size of the collective is inversely proportional to the strength of character of those pathetic individual weaklings of whom the group is composed. The smaller the character of the talking ape in question, the larger the colony among which you are likely to find it shrieking and flinging its feces. Those who boast of their numbers, do so as a means of confessing their inadequacies and uselessness as individual persons. What kind of imbecile points to a crowd as evidence of his intrinsic worth? If you ever find yourself identifying a race, ethnicity, nation, or religious group as the centerpiece of *your* identity, or of *your* value, then go the full distance and have yourself ground up and ingested by the masses with whom you claim to identify. Become *truly* a part of the whole—by virtue of your annihilation. You will eventually become part of the feces that the other apes in your collective fling at each other. Quite the accomplishment, is it not?

17 You shall not covet your neighbor's house. You shall not covet
your neighbor's wife, or his manservant or maidservant, or
his ox or donkey, or anything that belongs to your neighbor.

18 All the people witnessed the thunder and lightning, the
sound of the trumpet, and the mountain in smoke. And when
the people saw this, they trembled and stood at a distance.
19 "Speak to us yourself and we will listen," they said to Moses.
"But do not let God speak to us, or we will die."

20 "Do not be afraid," Moses replied. "For God has come to test
you, so that the fear of Him may be before you, to keep you
from sinning." 21 And the people stood at a distance as Moses
approached the thick darkness where God was.

Exodus 20

Scripture tells us that it is a sin to covet, but you know that coveting is both irrational and unhealthy, irrespective of any commands issued from God's throne. To desire what you do not have, and to desire it, moreover, so intensely that you are willing to take it by force from its rightful possessor (this latter element being the *heart* of coveting), betrays a subordination of your decency to your desire for material goods, political power, or economic advantage. You know that decency and virtue are infinitely more valuable than any object or condition for which you might consider trading them away. Virtue is not for sale. It cannot be purchased. It is, quite literally, *priceless*. You know that you are far better off with good character and with your dignity intact, than you could ever be with any amount of money, fame, or power purchased at the expense of shattered virtue and degraded personhood. A wealthy miscreant is a miscreant nonetheless. A politically powerful villain is no less villainous merely for residing in a Governor's mansion or holding a seat in the Senate. A captain of industry, who ascended the corporate ladder by "virtue" of corruption, should marinate in shame and steep in ignominy. Do not trade the greater and more abiding good for the lesser material benefit. The citadel is not properly abandoned for a night at the saloon. Rectitude. Self-discipline. Decency is not a negotiable good.

8 Jerusalem has sinned greatly;
therefore she has become an object of scorn.
All who honored her now despise her,
for they have seen her nakedness;
she herself groans and turns away.

9 Her uncleanness stains her skirts;
she did not consider her end.
Her downfall was astounding;
there was no one to comfort her.
Look, O LORD, on my affliction,
for the enemy has triumphed!

10 The adversary has seized
all her treasures.
For she has seen the nations
enter her sanctuary—
those You had forbidden
to enter Your assembly.

Lamentations 1

The end of your story never recedes, but rather approaches relentlessly. You will never have more time *left* than you have at this moment. You will never be younger than you are right now. Your death is closer right now than it has ever been before. The point is trivial and obvious, but do you take heed of its implications? What is it that you hope to accomplish? What manner of person do you hope to become? You know that time is running out. Yet—here you are. If *this* has been your overarching goal, if your current state of character is what you have been aiming at all along, you have set the bar inexcusably *low*, have you not? If your goals are all achieved, you may as well be done with the business of breathing in and out, having no particular purpose left to serve. Take to one of the many readily available exits. If, on the other hand, you have left a great deal yet undone (and you *must* admit that you have done so), then note the onrushing horizon, and bend all of your efforts at the business before you—right *now*! Stop your fiddling and frittering. Forward. Do not allow yourself a single backward step or a moment of hesitation.

17 And to Adam He said:

"Because you have listened to the voice of your wife
and have eaten of the tree
from which I commanded you not to eat,
cursed is the ground because of you;
through toil you will eat of it
all the days of your life.
18 Both thorns and thistles it will yield you,
and you will eat the plants of the field.
19 By the sweat of your brow
you will eat your bread,
until you return to the ground—
because out of it were you taken.
For dust you are,
and to dust you shall return."

20 And Adam named his wife Eve, because she would become
the mother of all the living.

Genesis 3

Do not allow your mind to despise or disdain the "little things." What, after all, is so grand about *you* that you manage to conjure contempt for "lesser concerns," or the "mundane" elements of the human condition? Everything you encounter contains at least a bit of a mystery—provided that you allow yourself to consider the relatedness of all things in the vast matrix of events that make up a life, and that constitute this world in which you find yourself embedded. Were you not a mere zygote, a microscopic, single-celled organism, in the not-so-distant past? Were you not a nonexistent nothing in particular before you were conceived? Will your body not expire, decay, disintegrate, and return again "unto the dust" from which *all* life came? A creature on a journey "from dust to dust" really ought not think too highly of itself or, more importantly, regard anything else as unworthy of its attention. Pay attention even to the "little things," and know that *you* are one of them. You are a tiny, ephemeral being with occasional delusions of grandeur. Humility. You are not worthy of reverence. Find something other than yourself that *is* worthy. Revere it.

7 The path of the righteous is level;
You clear a straight path for the righteous.
8 Yes, we wait for You, O LORD;
we walk in the path of Your judgments.
Your name and renown
are the desire of our souls.
9 My soul longs for You in the night;
indeed, my spirit within me diligently seeks You.
For when Your judgments come upon the earth,
the inhabitants of the world will learn righteousness.
10 Though grace is shown to the wicked man,
he does not learn righteousness.
In the land of righteousness he acts unjustly
and fails to see the majesty of the LORD.

Isaiah 26

Each morning, admonish yourself that you are *not* to complain today—about *anything*. You are to embrace each day as an unearned opportunity to draw breath, experience a world not of your making, and to learn something of which you had previously been ignorant. Every day constitutes an opportunity that is not available to nonhuman animals, who cannot reason about their condition, and each day is yours to experience due to, at least in part, sufficient luck to have survived this long. Not every person has been equally fortunate. Remember that. Should you fail to learn anything on any given day, know that the failure is *yours*, and is not properly laid at the feet of Fate, circumstances, or any alleged malevolent force outside of your own will. What condition, apart from death or acute dementia, can prohibit you from attending to events like a reasoning being in pursuit of understanding? Can your occupation not serve also as a field of novel inquiry? Does time spent with family preclude your attempts to know them better and to learn what occupies their minds? They are worthy of your attention and your interest. Does illness prevent you from understanding the experience of illness? Pay attention. Keep learning until you drop dead. After that, perhaps you will get to rest.

1 Call out if you please, but who will answer?
To which of the holy ones will you turn?
2 For resentment kills a fool,
and envy slays the simple.
3 I have seen a fool taking root,
but suddenly his house was cursed.
4 His sons are far from safety,
crushed in court without a defender.
5 The hungry consume his harvest,
taking it even from the thorns;
and the thirsty pant after his wealth.
6 For distress does not spring from the dust,
and trouble does not sprout from the ground.
7 Yet man is born to trouble
as surely as sparks fly upward.

Job 5

Envy is a filthy, degrading, and self-destructive habit of the mind. It is no accident that covetousness is the one "thought crime" prohibited by the Ten Commandments. One who covets his neighbor's goods is less than a hop, skip, and jump removed from the thief, the adulterer, or even the murderer. These misdeeds are the gruesome culmination of the misbegotten coveting that scripture proscribes. These sinful deeds originate in the prohibited desire to take those things that are not rightfully yours for the taking and that rightfully belong to someone else or, perhaps, rightfully belong to no one—and ought to remain in no human's possession. The envious mind gives birth to the thieving hands and feet. Covetousness impels the body toward ignoble goals and actions. If the mind stays clear of vicious, malevolent thoughts, the hands and feet are left with only virtuous deeds to enact. The words of an envious mind's mouth are poisonous, malodorous, and ignoble. Words prompted by a lust for your neighbor's holdings are unworthy of anyone more virtuous than a begging mongrel, or a slithering snake. Indeed, the dog is, at least, more honest about his desires than is the conniving wretch. A dog will look you in the eye as it begs for a morsel. Do not allow yourself to be less honorable than a canine.

10Then say to them, "This is what the LORD of Hosts, the God
of Israel, says: I will send for My servant Nebuchadnezzar
king of Babylon, and I will set his throne over these stones
that I have embedded, and he will spread his royal pavilion
over them. 11He will come and strike down the land of Egypt,
bringing death to those destined for death, captivity to those
destined for captivity, and the sword to those destined for
the sword.

12I will kindle a fire in the temples of the gods of Egypt, and
he will burn those temples and take their gods as captives.
So he will wrap himself with the land of Egypt as a shepherd
wraps himself in his garment, and he will depart from there
unscathed.

13He will demolish the sacred pillars of the temple of the sun
in Egypt, and he will burn down the temples of the gods of
Egypt."

Jeremiah 43

Do not drive thoughts of your death, or of bodily injury, or of other forms of disability, too roughly or too quickly out of your mind. You should not obsess or perseverate on matters lying beyond your control, of course, and fantasizing about immortality is largely, if not entirely, a waste of time and energy. Recognize that you must consider the "dark" and potentially disturbing possibilities with a clear, sober mind. Perhaps there is a good deal to be learned from careful attention to the psychological and emotional states that tend to arise when the specter of death rears its head, or when the inevitability of your decline thrusts itself into your consciousness. The ages and the ancients have advised humans to "Know thyself." *Do* you? If fear is your initial response to such considerations, perhaps you regard your life thus far as inadequate in some fashion. Perhaps the inevitable end of your life fills you with anxiety about all that you have failed to accomplish and failed to learn. What is it that you believe you are missing? In what way can you make yourself whole? Do what is necessary to be able to embrace your death with equanimity when your time comes. Is this not also an embrace of your *life*? If death scares you, then that is an indication that you are troubled by your inadequacies, and by the dearth of your accomplishments. In other words, it is your *life* that troubles you. So, get to work on becoming worthy of a serene death.

16 A wise man fears and turns from evil,
but a fool is careless and reckless.

17 A quick-tempered man acts foolishly,
and a devious man is hated.

18 The simple inherit folly,
but the prudent are crowned with knowledge.

19 The evil bow before the good,
and the wicked at the gates of the righteous.

Proverbs 14

Your character is *your* responsibility, and it ought to be your primary concern in everything that you do, everything that you say, and every thought that you allow yourself to think. Do not so much as entertain any possible action that would diminish your moral status. Jettison any sentimentality in this area, and leave all childish musings in the past. Blame no one else. Do not rail against circumstance. Take responsibility for *everything* that lies within your control, and respond to all that lies *beyond* your control after the fashion of a reasonable and honorable agent in pursuit of wisdom. Make no excuses for your failures. Accept no excuses offered by others on your behalf. Turn them away and make it clear that you have no interest in fables proffered to soothe your ego. If someone imputes false motives to you, say nothing in response. Let them claim whatever they wish to claim about the contents of your mind. What business of yours is their error in judgment? If someone blames you for conditions beyond your control, so be it. Let them describe the world in whatever manner suits their purposes. Nod in agreement if you like. Your ancestors have sinned, and you are held to account for misdeeds committed before you were born? Fine. Let it be so. Embrace the blame. Wear it like a shield. This *is* within your power. Wink at Fate. Grin at false accusations. Laugh at foolishness.

7 The days of punishment have come;
the days of retribution have arrived—
let Israel know it.
The prophet is called a fool,
and the inspired man insane,
because of the greatness
of your iniquity and hostility.
8 The prophet is Ephraim's watchman,
along with my God,
yet the snare of the fowler lies on all his paths.
Hostility is in the house of his God!
9 They have deeply corrupted themselves
as in the days of Gibeah;
He will remember their guilt;
He will punish their sins.

Hosea 9

See to it that you do not cultivate artificial "needs," that can serve only to impoverish you spiritually and lead to depravity in their pursuit. Your desires must also be kept fairly simple and constrained by nature and reason. If you find yourself wanting some experience that requires behaviors that are contrary to your own flourishing in accordance with nature's "way," then you ought to extirpate that desire. Nature has supplied you with needs and desires aplenty. Do not invent desiderata to occupy your limited time, attention, and resources. How pathetic is it to "need" a cigarette, or a dose of some illicit narcotic? A need that conduces to the destruction of mind, body, and spirit is a multilayered perversion, and the voluntary adoption of an unhealthy addiction is nothing short of shameful. If you fall into such a trap of your own making, you should not expect sympathy from anyone and, moreover, you are entitled to precisely *no* self-pity or forgiveness. Thrust the dark habit away from you with every iota of will that you can still muster. If this is insufficient, then your final thought ought to be, "You did this to yourself, dummy." That is no way to end your experiences on this planet. Do not "go out" with regret and self-recrimination. Hopefully, your last thought can be worthy of a rational person who faces the completion of a life worth living.

May

21 A voice is heard on the barren heights,
the children of Israel weeping and begging for mercy,
because they have perverted their ways
and forgotten the LORD their God.

22 "Return, O faithless children,
and I will heal your faithlessness."

"Here we are. We come to You,
for You are the LORD our God.
23 Surely deception comes from the hills,
commotion from the mountains,
but surely the salvation of Israel
is in the LORD our God.
24 From our youth, that shameful god
has consumed what our fathers have worked for—
their flocks and herds,
their sons and daughters."

Jeremiah 3

The talking apes have gotten on your nerves again. Where do you place the blame? If you allowed yourself to expect civility from the simian hordes, then you have brought this irritation upon yourself. They shriek, leap about, and fling their feces because they can manage no better. This is all just behavior in accordance with their nature—a nature that you share with them, by the way. Consider the shrieking and leaping about that you have perpetrated in your time. Do not absolve *yourself*, ape. More importantly, you ought to know better than to demand propriety from those who have demonstrated neither any interest in it, nor even the capacity to understand or enact it. Why not set snails upon a piano keyboard and insist that they produce a symphony? Again and again you allow yourself to slip into disappointment with the world as it stands, and as you have known it to be since your childhood. What is your excuse for this recurring delusion? You reject reality in favor of fantasy. Are you a child? It is time to put aside childish expectations and the insistence that the world and its inhabitants must be other than they are. No one died and made you King of the Talking Primates. You command no one other than yourself, and you do *that* only rather poorly.

10 My shield is with God,
who saves the upright in heart.
11 God is a righteous judge
and a God who feels indignation each day.

12 If one does not repent,
God will sharpen His sword;
He has bent and strung His bow.
13 He has prepared His deadly weapons;
He ordains His arrows with fire.

Psalm 7

In its fundamentals, the human condition does not change. The challenges facing Pythagoras, Socrates, Diogenes, Aristotle, the Buddha, Confucius, Sun Tzu, and Moses, are morally, psychologically, and emotionally much the same as the challenges you face today—although your *material* needs are *far* more easily satisfied than were theirs. You have access to technological advancements that would have seemed miraculous to ancient peoples. The information at your fingertips probably outstrips the total accumulated knowledge of the entire human race just a few centuries ago. These are not, however, intrinsic features of the human animal, and you are not superior to the ancients merely because you can access an Internet search engine or take an antibiotic. As for the struggle to become a decent human being, to govern yourself wisely, and to coauthor a human life worthy of anyone's notice—your mission is not different in kind from the missions of your forebears. What then is your excuse for your comparative weakness, your inveterate failure, and your ceaseless self-pity? Are you simply a whining, weak, failure of a human being? If there is nothing more to be said for your life, then you may as well end it expeditiously. You are something of an embarrassment, are you not? If there is more to you than that, get about the business of demonstrating it. Your life *is* your work of art. The work is, as yet, unfinished. You have no idea how much time is left to you. Enough has been frittered away. Stop dawdling. Work.

4"Then you will know that I have sent you this commandment,
that My covenant with Levi may continue," says the LORD of
Hosts. 5"My covenant with him was one of life and peace, and
I gave them to him; it called for reverence, and he revered Me
and stood in awe of My name.

6True instruction was in his mouth, and nothing false
was found on his lips. He walked with Me in peace and
uprightness, and he turned many from iniquity. 7For the lips
of a priest should preserve knowledge, and people should
seek instruction from his mouth, because he is the messenger
of the LORD of Hosts."

Malachi 2

Fairness is a fool's desire, and only a child or a lunatic expects life to be fair. Nothing about the natural world has *ever* been fair, and the "civilized" world is, at best, *designed* with something like fairness in mind—and none of the "powers that be" have ever taken the pursuit of fairness very seriously. If you ever find yourself bemoaning the fact that you have been treated unfairly, you should render judgment against *yourself* immediately. *You* are delusional. *You* are the problem. *You* have allowed yourself to develop expectations that conform neither to reality, nor to any persons with whom you have ever had contact—including yourself. You struggle to recall a single occasion on which you have behaved in a manner that was scrupulously fair to all involved parties, not to mention an occasion on which the alleged fairness was *motivated* by principled moral convictions. In other words, you may have been fair as a matter of happenstance, but *not* as a natural outflow of virtuous inclination. In any event, what is the great benefit allegedly associated with fair treatment? Perhaps it is a means of avoiding unnecessary suffering. Do you shun hardship, misery, and injustice even though you believe these experiences to be the greatest opportunities to develop wisdom, self-discipline, and virtuous character? How serious then are you about improving yourself? Suffering works. Suffering is a very effective method of self-improvement. Suffer.

24A man's steps are from the LORD,
so how can anyone understand his own way?

25It is a trap for a man to dedicate something rashly
only later to reconsider his vows.

26A wise king separates out the wicked
and drives the threshing wheel over them.

Proverbs 20

There is no such thing as a partial commitment, a half-hearted oath, or a moderately serious vow. You are utterly committed in heart, mind, soul, and sinew, or you are a disingenuous play-actor, unworthy of anyone's trust—including your own. Your wedding vows, for example, are not to be treated as contingencies, or as, in *any* way, dependent upon circumstance or passing impulses. It simply makes *no* difference that things change, time passes, other people move in and out of your general vicinity, etc. Marriage is for *life*, or it is a sham. Decide, in advance, that no "temptation" is to be taken seriously or even momentarily contemplated. There is *no* human being whom you can encounter that has the capacity to cause you to waver, even for an instant, where your commitment to your spouse is concerned. In this area, there are no further decisions to be made. You will *not* be an adulterer, you will *not* abuse your spouse, and you will *not* allow any interest to jeopardize your marriage, no matter what contingencies may arise. *All* vows are to be treated in like fashion. When you make a promise, you will fulfill that promise or you will accept the shame that ought to ensue when you fail to do the right thing even though doing the right thing is entirely within your power. This entails that you are never to make a promise that necessitates anything occurring that is outside of the sphere of your direct control. Do not allow profligacy to infect your promises. Your word *is* your bond. Virtuous bonds are *not* to be broken—though the heavens fall.

1The fool says in his heart,
"There is no God."
They are corrupt; their acts are vile.
There is no one who does good.

2The LORD looks down from heaven
upon the sons of men
to see if any understand,
if any seek God.
3All have turned away,
they have together become corrupt;
there is no one who does good,
not even one.

Psalm 14

About what do you allow yourself to fret this day? Are you concerned about the potential outcome of some election, or of some financial consideration or other? Really? This is *none* of your business, as it lies beyond the control of your will and your power of choice. Your nation and its culture will be impacted, you are told? What of it? Impose some outcome by fiat, if you can. Oh, you cannot. Leave it aside then. Your culture is increasingly sick, perverse, depraved, and ignoble in every significant facet of its evolution (or devolution)? Again, what of it? Compel the contrary developments in each matter that concerns you. Once again, you cannot. What do you mean by allowing despair to creep into your consciousness over events that are none of your business, and about which you can do nothing at all. Turn away from emotional entanglements with any and all conditions that do not obey your will—including other persons, their beliefs, their behavior, and the course of their lives. If other persons are ignoble, vicious, or otherwise disreputable, that is *their* concern. Are *you* ignoble in some fashion or other? If so, devote yourself to ceasing the objectionable behavior, and inculcating its opposite inclination. Bend your efforts upon ennobling *your* character irrespective of the surrounding culture. You are *not* everyone. Stop pretending that you command anyone or anything other than yourself. You need not, and *should* not, try to "be everyone." Can you not, at least, try to be *someone*?

8 Now Hezekiah had asked Isaiah, "What is the sign that the LORD will heal me and that I will go up to the house of the LORD on the third day?"

9 And Isaiah replied, "This will be a sign to you from the LORD that He will do what He has promised: Would you like the shadow to go forward ten steps, or back ten steps?"

10 "It is easy for the shadow to lengthen ten steps," answered Hezekiah, "but not for it to go back ten steps."

11 So Isaiah the prophet called out to the LORD, and He brought the shadow back the ten steps it had descended on the stairway of Ahaz.

2 Kings 20

Scour off the encrustations of self-pity and despair, stop the whining about your life, and the pining for some silly idealization, and get to the business of constructing a worthy character for yourself. Either that, or point yourself in the direction of depravity and dissolution, run wildly into that abyss, and remove yourself from the lives of those who deserve better from you. If you do not recognize that you owe it to yourself and your Creator (if, indeed, there *is* a Creator) to try your best to live a virtuous life, do you not, at the very least, wish to be a virtuous and useful spouse, parent, and friend to those who occupy these roles in your life? Become a decent, virtuous human being, or get yourself gone from the lives of others—if not from life entirely. What is this pathetic, middling dance of mediocrity in which you seem ceaselessly to indulge? Must two steps of backsliding into moral weakness and degenerate lassitude follow *one* step in the direction of wisdom and nobility, always? Is progress really so unwelcome that you must see it undone before you can experience even *one* full moment of earned self-respect? A child is more diligent at play than you are at the only work that matters. Are you not more responsible for your development than is a child? You had better get to work on yourself. It must be forward and *only* forward for you.

29 The earth quakes and writhes
because the LORD's intentions against Babylon stand:
to make the land of Babylon a desolation,
without an inhabitant.
30 The warriors of Babylon have stopped fighting;
they sit in their strongholds.
Their strength is exhausted;
they have become like women.
Babylon's homes have been set ablaze,
the bars of her gates are broken.
31 One courier races to meet another,
and messenger follows messenger,
to announce to the king of Babylon
that his city has been captured from end to end.
32 The fords have been seized,
the marshes set on fire,
and the soldiers are terrified.

Jeremiah 51

Freedom of association is an underappreciated liberty, as is its corollary, freedom *from* association—with anyone whom you find to be despicable, stupid, or otherwise unworthy of your time and company. Epictetus warned against associating too frequently with those who are moral or intellectual inferiors. Those who do not "bring out the best in you" are a waste of your time, effort, energy, and life. Associating with lesser beings is like consorting with lepers or vampires. Diogenes found almost no one with whom he was willing to develop any deep or lasting relationship. Why would a man of his moral stature, his phenomenal strength of will, and his incorruptible spirit, sully himself by any sustained proximity with weaklings, imbeciles, psychological hemophiliacs, or moral invertebrates? An exemplar of dignity does not tolerate any unnecessary association with the commoner or the dullard. Your moral improvement will prove incompatible with the company of those to whom questions of character are alien or anachronistic. Many people seem to believe that concern with virtue and wisdom constitutes a quaint personality quirk. Those people are no better than parasites. Treat them like bloodsuckers.

20 "For long ago you broke your yoke
and tore off your chains,
saying, 'I will not serve!'
Indeed, on every high hill
and under every green tree
you lay down as a prostitute.
21 I had planted you like a choice vine
from the very best seed.
How could you turn yourself before me,
into a rotten wild vine?
22 Although you wash with lye
and use an abundance of soap,
the stain of your guilt is still before Me..."

Jeremiah 2

Evidence of civilizational collapse is mounting on every visible area across the horizon. You find it astonishing that there are people who do not perceive this, or who, in any event, do not admit that they perceive this. The West is dying. Indeed, the West is in fairly precipitous decline. The death of the West is, for reasons that you find difficult to fathom, largely a matter of ethno-suicide and cultural self-immolation. It seems that the West *wants* to die. There is something, evidently, hollow at the heart of contemporary Western populations. Perhaps the "death of God," about which Nietzsche wrote so vividly and presciently, has left the West unmoored from its heritage, and rendered it susceptible to the deadly siren's songs of relativism, secularism, and degenerate post-modernism. Perhaps decades of decadence have rendered Westerners soft, corrupt, and credulous. Perhaps a once noble and admirable cultural experiment has simply run its course and spent its vital energies. Cultural syphilis left unchecked and untreated, maybe? Nietzsche might have had a passing acquaintance with something along these lines.

Every living organism must die eventually, after all. It is, however, peculiar to witness this voluntary, passive slouching past Gomorrah, and into the abyss that stares back as the West plunges into it. This is, at the very least, something very sad. Where is the rage against the dying of *this* light? Where is the blood? If the West dies without "firing a shot," so to speak, then perhaps it deserves its fate.

14"Then I will enslave you to your enemies
in a land you do not know,
for My anger will kindle a fire
that will burn against you."

15You understand, O LORD;
remember me and attend to me.
Avenge me against my persecutors.
In Your patience, do not take me away.
Know that I endure reproach for Your honor.
16Your words were found, and I ate them.
Your words became a delight to me
and my heart's delight,
for I bear Your name,
O LORD God of Hosts.

Jeremiah 15

Witnessing the death of anyone you once loved, or anything with which you once felt a deep kinship, an allegiance, is emotionally and psychologically challenging for you. You need not deny this difficulty, nor pretend that the pain is unreal or chimerical. It is, indeed, all *too* real. Decay, dissolution, and death are inevitable. All that *is* shall eventually pass into all that *was*. No good will come of simply averting your eyes, or trying to wish the inevitable away. Facts do not obey your insistence to their contrary. When you see the moribund raising its head, when you perceive death's irreversibility, when you become aware that alternatives are not on offer, you are obligated to accept and embrace the inevitable as it approaches. If it is your own, then you are to allow death to wash over you and carry you where it will—without kicking, screaming, or offering even a moment of resistance. If the death that approaches is *not* yours, then you must acknowledge it, take appropriate note, engage in a suitable period of mourning (if it is appropriate to do so), and then move forward. Always move forward, until the death *is* yours. After that, advice is largely epiphenomenal.

10 Such punishment is specially reserved for those who indulge
the corrupt desires of the flesh and despise authority. Bold
and self-willed, these men are unafraid to slander angelic
majesties.
11 Yet not even angels, though greater in strength
and power, dare to bring such slanderous charges against
them before the Lord.

12 These men are like irrational animals, creatures of instinct,
born to be captured and destroyed. They blaspheme in
matters they do not understand, and like such creatures, they
too will be destroyed.
13 The harm they will suffer is the wages
of their wickedness.

2 Peter 2

The imbeciles have spoken once again. The speaking is, as usual, both loud and relentless. There is no cause for surprise here, is there? This is precisely what imbeciles do best and most insistently, is it not? Let them yap as they please, and resist the urge to vent spleen about the matter. Do them no harm. Were it not for their blather, you would have less opportunity to improve your powers of forbearance. A mighty, but stupid, opponent is properly used to strengthen your will, steel your resolve, and broaden the sphere of circumstances within which you are able to maintain your equanimity. Morons offer an opportunity to learn the rational, mature methods of dealing with morons. You should not take that away from them, after all. If you can retain your serenity even when you are surrounded by those most dearly, and vocally, devoted to idiocy and inanity, then surely you can maintain dignified calm in the presence of the merely mundane, the vapidly quotidian, or the vaguely irritating details of the average day in the life of a talking ape trying to walk erect for a short while. It is worth noting, that no one ever promised you a "rose garden" devoid of dimwits. It is the apes and not the angels among whom you make your home. Be, at the very least, an ape with a contented disposition. Are there insufficient bananas for your liking? Do you lack tree branches upon which to swing to and fro? Find food and shelter, acquire sustenance, and try to find a mate. That is enough. Let the others posture and groom each other as they please. Let them shriek. This is nothing to you.

1"Come, all of you who thirst,
come to the waters;
and you without money,
come, buy, and eat!
Come, buy wine and milk,
without money and without cost!
2Why spend money on that which is not bread,
and your labor on that which does not satisfy?
Listen carefully to Me, and eat what is good,
and your soul will delight in the richest of foods."

Isaiah 55

There seems to be a great deal of yammering about money and all that money can buy, does there not? Perhaps a bit of puzzlement at the fact that money can buy so much is warranted, but that can wait. Those who insist that others are "greedy" seem awfully adamant that the redistribution of the largesse, and of presumably ill-gotten wealth, will be of great benefit to society at large. How, though, does spreading further and wider the object of the greed that is so objectionable improve the common lot? Surely, the greedy will be less satisfied having been stripped of the object of their desire. Is their misery a proper societal goal? Is it an *intrinsic* moral good? On the other end of the exchange, the recipients of the redistributed "excess" are intended to profit from an increased share of the very object of objectionably greedy desire in those from whom it was altruistically stripped. Giving the *filthy money* to the poor is good for them, evidently. They desire it, after all. Is this *not* a manifestation of greed? If the wealthy want to keep their money, that is avarice. If the poor want to receive money taken from the wealthy, that is also avarice, is it not? Is dangling money before the poor not an inducement to the very greed that is the vice allegedly justifying the vilification of the wealthy? Encouraging class envy is *not* a noble endeavor. Rich people never stole any money from *you*. Yet, you are supposed to resent their wealth, and demand its transfer to you, for some reason? This is not even a coherent narrative anymore. Avert your eyes from this lunacy if you must—but you will, thereby, miss a fascinating show.

> 5 Then the LORD saw that the wickedness of man was great
> upon the earth, and that every inclination of the thoughts
> of his heart was altogether evil all the time. 6 And the LORD
> regretted that He had made man on the earth, and it grieved
> Him in His heart. 7 So the LORD said, "I will blot out man,
> whom I have created, from the face of the earth—every man
> and beast and crawling creature and bird of the air—for I am
> grieved that I have made them."
>
> Genesis 6

If you do not concern yourself with your cat's opinion of your character, and you really should *not* do so, what excuse do you offer for allowing yourself any preoccupation with what your colleagues, relatives, or neighbors think of you? Your colleagues, relatives, and neighbors are, presumably, wiser and more perceptive than your cat. Of course, you do not wish to be presumptuous about such matters, and some persons in the categories indicated seem to work fairly assiduously to prove the contrary. In any event, the benefit of the doubt is not unreasonable. Perhaps that is the most felicitous attitude in this instance. Do not presume. After all, when have you known your cat to burn the roof of his mouth biting into a slice of pizza too soon? Nearly every human being you have ever met has made this mistake repeatedly. *You* are a repeat offender in this regard, are you not? Nonetheless, suppose that the humans, the talking primates of your acquaintance, *are,* in fact, intellectually superior to your stupid cat—the one that you step on several times each day. Does this give the humans' opinion of you some special purchase upon your imagination? The contents of their minds are entrusted by God, or by nature, to them—and you ought not concern yourself with anything not entrusted to you. What rattles around in their heads need not be any problem for you. Such concerns are, to say the least, unbecoming. Be more like your cat insofar as disregard for humanity is concerned. Better to bat about a ball of yarn than to investigate the ruminations of imbeciles. In the former case, you might get to keep some yarn.

12But many of the older priests, Levites, and family heads
who had seen the first temple wept loudly when they saw the
foundation of this temple. Still, many others shouted joyfully.
13The people could not distinguish the shouts of joy from the
sound of weeping, because the people were making so much
noise. And the sound was heard from afar.

Ezra 3

The rejection of individualism is a manifestation of a despicable herd instinct, and democracy is the delusion that a majority of the flock is morally entitled to impose its communal stupidity upon the minority. The mere prevalence or preponderance of an opinion is hardly evidence of its truth, utility, or virtue. History is littered with popular idiocies. This planet was not flat merely because nearly everyone believed it to be so. It was also never at the center of the universe simply because it appeared so to the masses. An evil spirit assailing your body and mind does not cause your respiratory maladies. The list of broadly embraced stupidities could continue, but the point is made, is it not? Consider the contemporary films that gross the most at the box office, the most popular television programs, or the general moral and intellectual character of those representatives elected by the people. How much more evidence is required to convince you that you travel aboard a ship of fools. The sprawling crew has no idea where the ship is headed, and they cannot be trusted to chart a course anywhere. A large number of herd animals bleating more or less in unison, and doing so in vague proximity to your place of residence, is hardly a reason to bleat along with the masses. It is less reason still to obey the dictates of the bovine, the ovine, or the primate collectives, when those sentiments are contrary to reason (flawed though this faculty may be). The multitudes may set the agenda in a democracy, and there may be legal authority attached to the will of the majority—but you are free to ignore, ridicule, or silently condemn that authority as you see fit, or as reason dictates. Let the masses hang. Let them dangle. What is this to you?

7So I pastured the flock marked for slaughter, especially the
afflicted of the flock. Then I took for myself two staffs, calling
one Favor and the other Union, and I pastured the flock. 8And
in one month I dismissed three shepherds.

My soul grew impatient with the flock, and their souls also
detested me. 9Then I said, "I will no longer shepherd you. Let
the dying die, and the perishing perish; let the rest devour
one another's flesh."

Zechariah 11

Your lack of charity toward yourself is understandable. Anyone who had been compelled to spend as much time with *you* as you have spent in your own company would be sick and tired of your inveterate stupidity and your relentless internal yammering. The complaints seem to ricochet about the innards of your skull, and there seems to be fairly little to obstruct the reverberation. Of course you find yourself irritating! Who can blame you? Your uncharitable disposition toward others, however, has not been quite so well earned. Why the impatience with others who are as stupid, incompetent, and lazy as you? You are *far* from free of these faults, and yet you seethe when you encounter them in others. You manage to be taken aback and irritated by bungling. What do you expect from talking apes wearing shoes? Do you expect the human world to be peopled by saints and intellectual exemplars? Apes cannot even *tie* shoelaces. By the way, *your* shoes are sometimes untied, are they not? In fact, it is probably worth your while to check your laces right now. You have wasted far more than your fair share of time (whatever the individual allotment designated for waste), and certainly far more of your time than anyone else has the capacity to waste on your behalf. Learn to walk upright before castigating the other primates. People who live in glasses houses should not fling their feces.

Well, *no one* should do *that*. Also, be mindful of where you throw stones.

12“Do not be afraid, Daniel,” he said, “for from the first day
that you purposed to understand and to humble yourself
before your God, your words were heard, and I have come
in response to them. 13However, the prince of the kingdom of
Persia opposed me for twenty-one days. Then Michael, one
of the chief princes, came to help me, for I had been left there
with the kings of Persia. 14Now I have come to explain to you
what will happen to your people in the latter days, for the
vision concerns those days.”

15While he was speaking these words to me, I set my face
toward the ground and became speechless. 16And suddenly
one with the likeness of a man touched my lips, and I opened
my mouth and said to the one standing before me, “My lord,
because of the vision, I am overcome with anguish, and I have
no strength. 17How can I, your servant, speak with you, my
lord? Now I have no strength, nor is any breath left in me.”

Daniel 10

Your obsession with possible future travails and potential calamities borders on the ludicrous, and is thoroughly unhealthy as well as counterproductive. Instead of your perseveration about disasters not yet incurred, many of which, upon the slightest analysis, prove to be wildly unlikely, you might focus your attention upon the actual present and the immediate job at hand. The more you take care of current duties and obligations properly, the more you might obviate unpleasant contingencies allegedly lying in wait over the horizon. Many of the bogeymen that populate your darkest imaginations would evaporate if you just took care of that small portion of the present that lies within your direct, unmediated control. Take care of your mind, your attention, and your responsibilities, and relinquish morbid curiosity about matters that are none of your proper concern. Dread of possible, and mostly counterfactual, futures is an indication of ingratitude for the wonders available *right now*. Breathe in. Breathe out. Note that you have eyes with which to see, ears with which to hear, and a faculty of reason that (occasionally) allows you to contemplate the astonishing world around you. That is enough. Right *now* is enough. You had, in any event, better hope so. *Now*… is all you are ever going to get. Pay attention, right *now*.

June

7 Submit yourselves, then, to God. Resist the devil, and he will
flee from you. 8 Draw near to God, and He will draw near
to you. Cleanse your hands, you sinners, and purify your
hearts, you double-minded. 9 Grieve, mourn, and weep. Turn
your laughter to mourning, and your joy to gloom. 10 Humble
yourselves before the Lord, and He will exalt you.

James 4

Heraclitus allegedly wept at the stupidity, corruption, and hopelessness of the human race. Democritus, we are told, laughed at the people he encountered because he regarded them and their behavior as absurd and silly. Perhaps there is something to be said for both of these perspectives. There *is* genuine villainy in mankind, and "man's inhumanity toward man" has wrought genuine suffering in abundance nearly beyond imagining. Of course, the merely ludicrous has never been in short supply where human interaction is concerned. The self-importance, the pretense, and the childishness are ubiquitous, and all run as deep as the marrow in your bones. No one has complained about a dearth of stupidity and foolishness among members of your species. Human beings are like dimwitted bit players in a comedy, but they believe themselves to be leading characters in a drama or a tragedy. Rare is the talking ape that insists on being ignored or regarded as nothing more than a peripheral element of the background scenery. All seem to think that they are heroes and heroines in stories centering upon the events of their own lives. In fairly short order, all are reduced to worm food and dust. There is something odd about arrogant, self-centered worm food, is there not? Perhaps Heraclitus laughed himself to tears, and Democritus cackled in maniacal rage. Maybe there is less separating their perspectives than the laughing and the weeping might seem to indicate. In any event, some of the apes may laugh, and some of the apes may cry. Most do a fair share of each. Their reasons for so doing are their own. What is any of this to you? A talking ape makes noise with its face. This is hardly something new under the sun.

16 If you have understanding, hear this;
listen to my words.
17 Could one who hates justice govern?
Will you condemn the just and mighty One,
18 who says to kings, "You are worthless!"
and to nobles, "You are wicked,"
19 who is not partial to princes
and does not favor rich over poor?
For they are all the work of His hands.
20 They die in a moment, and at midnight;
the people convulse and pass away;
the mighty are removed without human hand.

Job 34

Do not turn away too quickly from the misfortunes of others. There is, quite often, less separating their experience from yours than might meet the eye. Even if you observe persons suffering something that you have not suffered and never will, it still behooves you to pay attention. You can learn better and worse methods of dealing with suffering by vicarious observation and the assistance of a well-trained imagination. What can happen to other persons, or something equally difficult and challenging, *can* happen to you and yours. There is no excuse for being stymied by shock or paralyzed by surprise when this or that eventuality befalls you. Did you not understand that you are of a like kind with the others? When death comes for you, and it *will*, do not be caught unawares as if you were ignorant of your own mortality. Surely, you have seen enough dead bodies to realize that they are not very different from your own. Your corpse will not be so easy to identify among a group of others, and your bones will be all but indistinguishable from the rest. Do not delude yourself about the comparative safety and security of your nation, or the durability of your culture. There is nothing special about your place and time. What are Athens, Sparta, and Rome today? None is at an apex. Where is Pharaoh's dominion today? The pyramids are mostly for tourism now. The West teeters even as you write these words. How much time remains for today's "empires"? This *too* shall pass away.

[1]Then I saw a new heaven and a new earth, for the first heaven
and earth had passed away, and the sea was no more. [2]I saw
the holy city, the new Jerusalem, coming down out of heaven
from God, prepared as a bride adorned for her husband.

[3]And I heard a loud voice from the throne saying:

"Behold, the dwelling place of God is with man,
and He will live with them.
They will be His people,
and God Himself will be with them as their God.
[4]He will wipe away every tear from their eyes,
and there will be no more death
or mourning or crying or pain,
for the former things have passed away."

[5]And the One seated on the throne said, "Behold, I make all
things new." Then He said, "Write this down, for these words
are faithful and true." [6]And He told me, "It is done! I am the
Alpha and the Omega, the Beginning and the End. To the
thirsty I will give freely from the spring of the water of life."

Revelation 21

The pain is fairly intense today. You woke up wincing. So, what of it? Wince, groan a bit if you cannot help yourself, and get about the business of the day. Were you promised a lifetime devoid of pain, suffering, and inconvenience? Were you unaware of physical frailties inherent in the human condition? You have no excuse for surprise or disappointment, and your complaints about the matter, though they are mostly internal, are entirely unjustified manifestations of petulance, weakness, and cowardice. You are not entitled to gripe about *anything*. Look at the life you have been granted. It is a gift, in some sense or other, is it not? You never earned life as a human being, in a wealthy nation, replete with technological advantages, did you? You won the lottery! You are *entitled* to nothing. You get what you get, and you had better learn to be grateful for *all* of it. The pain you feel now is but one part of the fullness of a tolerably lived human life. If you are unwilling to endure the pain, you have no business enjoying the pleasure. Furthermore, you really do take on an ugly countenance when you complain and whine. Try not to make yourself any more repulsive than you are by nature.

1 At that time Hannah prayed:

"My heart rejoices in the LORD
in whom my horn is exalted.
My mouth speaks boldly against my enemies,
for I rejoice in Your salvation.
2 There is no one holy like the LORD.
Indeed, there is no one besides You!
And there is no rock like our God.

3 Do not boast so proudly,
or let arrogance come from your mouth,
for the LORD is a God who knows,
and by Him actions are weighed.

4 The bows of the warriors are broken,
but the feeble are equipped with strength.
5 The well-fed hire themselves out for food,
but the starving hunger no more.
The barren woman gives birth to seven,
but she who has many sons pines away."

1 Samuel 2

You dare not tread upon ground that is properly reserved for beings more richly endowed with wisdom and virtue than you. Anthropocentric arrogance seems to lack any upper limit. *Your* hubris is certainly a significant contribution to the great steaming pile of human arrogance, is it not? Surely, you ought to recognize your limitations and heed the obvious implications. Where does anyone get the idea that the human brain, functioning at slightly higher levels of complexity than the orangutan brain, is capable of understanding and assimilating all information potentially available about the external world, and about the internal sphere of consciousness and cognition itself? This is a dangerous haughtiness. Of course, you ought to try to learn as much as you can, particularly information that is practically applicable to living a flourishing, virtuous life. Do not, however, mistake the capacity to reason with the Godlike ability to command the cosmos and know every sparrow's fall. The world is *not* centered upon *you*. Indeed, you are merely passing through. Try to cause as little damage as possible, and remember to be grateful for the journey. Mysteries are not always challenges, or puzzles beckoning you to solve them. Some mysteries are warnings. Learn when it is best to keep your distance.

12 And the LORD said to Moses, 13 "Tell the Israelites, 'Surely
you must observe My Sabbaths, for this will be a sign between
Me and you for the generations to come, so that you may
know that I am the LORD who sanctifies you. 14 Observe the
Sabbath, for it is holy to you. Everyone who profanes it must
surely be put to death. Whoever does work on that day must
be cut off from his people. 15 For six days work may be done,
but the seventh day must be a Sabbath of solemn rest, holy to
the LORD. Whoever does any work on the Sabbath day must
surely be put to death.

16 The Israelites must observe the Sabbath, celebrating it as
a lasting covenant for the generations to come. 17 It is a sign
between Me and the Israelites forever; for in six days the
LORD made the heavens and the earth, but on the seventh
day He rested and was refreshed.'"

Exodus 31

Do you set aside at least one day each week for devotion to family, friends, and considerations of the home life in general? Do you reserve time and energy for interpersonal relations and quiet contemplation? If not, you are voluntarily enslaving yourself to your career, to labor, and to the ceaseless acquisition of material gain. Of course, none of that material wealth travels with you beyond the grave. Perhaps *nothing* does. Certainly, though, the money stays here. All work and no play may "make Jack a dull boy," but all work and no time for family and friends, the very *point* of acquiring material benefit, makes you a lousy spouse, parent, companion, and citizen of the world. Call the day you set aside to do no work, and engage in no labor for money, a "Sabbath" if you are so inclined. Call it a "family day" if you prefer. In any event, give yourself, your time, and your vital energies to those who largely make your life worth living—

at *least* one day each week. No one ever regrets prioritizing love, family, and the things that really matter. No one ever lay on a deathbed bemoaning the fact that not enough of the life that is now ending was spent at the office, or commuting, or attending interminable and pointless meetings at work. It is both good and wise to devote time to other, more important, more sacred matters. Be at ease with this. Even God is said to have rested on the seventh day. Do not attempt to outwork the Lord.

11 Then Jesus said, "There was a man who had two sons. 12 The
younger son said to him, 'Father, give me my share of the
estate.' So he divided his property between them.

13 After a few days, the younger son got everything together
and journeyed to a distant country, where he squandered his
wealth in wild living.
14 After he had spent all he had, a severe famine swept through
that country, and he began to be in need. 15 So he went and
hired himself out to a citizen of that country, who sent him
into his fields to feed the pigs. 16 He longed to fill his belly
with the pods the pigs were eating, but no one would give
him a thing.
17 Finally he came to his senses and said, 'How many of my
father's hired servants have plenty of food? But here I am,
starving to death! 18 I will get up and go back to my father and
say to him, "Father, I have sinned against heaven and against
you. 19 I am no longer worthy to be called your son. Make me
like one of your hired servants."'
20 So he got up and went to his father. But while he was
still in the distance, his father saw him and was filled with
compassion. He ran to his son, embraced him, and kissed
him.
21 The son declared, 'Father, I have sinned against heaven and
against you. I am no longer worthy to be called your son.'
22 But the father said to his servants, 'Quick! Bring the best
robe and put it on him. Put a ring on his finger and sandals
on his feet. 23 Bring the fattened calf and kill it. Let us feast and
celebrate. 24 For this son of mine was dead and is alive again!
He was lost and is found!' So they began to celebrate."

Luke 15

The prodigal son left home because he had frittered away the many advantages and privileges provided to him. Shame drove him away. Many seem to misunderstand this bit of the lesson. He left *because* of his prodigality; he was not "prodigal" because he left home. He was welcomed home *despite* his prodigality, and he was treated like a son resurrected from the dead, because he had learned a lesson worth more than all of the material wealth he had carelessly frittered away. Consider your own time, money, and energy. Have you not been guilty of a similar heedlessness on more than one occasion? Have you not wasted resources, opportunity, and vitality, in pursuit of silly, frivolous, and ignoble ends? You do not know how much time remains for you. The hour draws near, and you have felt, for some time now, that yours will not be an especially long life. You can cite no good rationale for this feeling, but it remains with you nonetheless. The time for prodigality is long since past. Come home. Cease your carelessness. Wake up. Soon… may be too late.

7 When they continued to question Him, He straightened up
and said to them, "Let him who is without sin among you be
the first to cast a stone at her." 8 And again He bent down and
wrote on the ground.

9 When they heard this, they began to go away one by one,
beginning with the older ones, until only Jesus was left, with
the woman standing there. 10 Then Jesus straightened up and
asked her, "Woman, where are your accusers? Has no one
condemned you?"

11 "No one, Lord," she answered.

"Then neither do I condemn you," Jesus declared. "Now go and sin no more."

John 8

Jesus dared those "who are without sin" to cast the first stone, to harm a woman who was, perhaps, no worse a sinner than were the men he dared to assault her, and this is, indeed, a valuable lesson. You ought to be hesitant to accuse others, especially given the deep, abiding corruption lurking not so very far below the surface façade of civility that seems to be required for interpersonal relations. There is, however, a second lesson in Jesus' words on this occasion, and it is too frequently elided or forgotten. Jesus told the alleged adulteress to desist in committing this sin. He told her to do this "no more." He did not simply admonish those who would harm the woman, and the concern was not only with the hypocrisy of "stone throwers," but he also reminded the woman that she, too, is a sinner, and that her behavior, though not properly punishable by stoning at the hands of an angry and duplicitous mob, is not to be tolerated by the woman, herself. It is *not* permissible to engage in adultery. Jesus did not simply let the woman "off the hook," or merely regard her as a victim. He instructed her to work on the improvement of her *own* character. This type of effort is always within your power, and is your first proper concern. The admonition to "sin no more," or to, at the very least, do your best to avoid this type of conduct, is worthy of careful consideration. It seems like good advice, does it not?

[1]Now the Spirit expressly states that in later times some will
abandon the faith to follow deceitful spirits and the teachings
of demons, [2]influenced by the hypocrisy of liars, whose
consciences are seared with a hot iron.

[3]They will prohibit marriage and require abstinence from
certain foods that God has created to be received with
thanksgiving by those who believe and know the truth. [4]For
every creation of God is good, and nothing that is received
with thanksgiving should be rejected, [5]because it is sanctified
by the word of God and prayer.

1 Timothy 4

Your nation sets aside one day each year as an official celebration of Thanksgiving. How many citizens of your nation devote this day to sincere expressions of gratitude is anyone's guess, and almost certainly not worthy of investigation. This national gesture is wise and beneficial as far as it goes, but its scope is much too limited, and its proper motivation is all too easily lost, forgotten, or misplaced. All genuine gratitude, in the final analysis, must attach to the opportunity to exist *at all*—under *any* conditions. Standard objects of gratitude require relatively little intellectual effort. To be grateful for family, and food, and freedom, is not so challenging, is it? Indeed, it is somewhat puzzling that some of your fellow citizens manage, somehow, to express so *little* gratitude for the astonishing good fortune of being born in this place and at this point in history. How *do* they manage this species of boorishness? Stunning. It is, in any event, gratitude for suffering, for injustice, for the dark nights that disquiet even the noblest souls, it is giving thanks for the chance *even* to experience *these*, that marks the strongest will and the most elevated states of character. Can you give thanks for your broken bones, your torn ligaments, your heartbreak, and your seemingly ubiquitous and ever-expanding aches and pains? Remember that you *earned* neither bones nor breath. Who told you that you were entitled to a body that does not break, does not age, and does not deteriorate? The world is not a playground and you are not a child. Do not embrace childish or irrational expectations.

1 To everything there is a season,
and a time for every purpose under heaven:
2 a time to be born and a time to die,
a time to plant and a time to uproot,
3 a time to kill and a time to heal,
a time to break down and a time to build,
4 a time to weep and a time to laugh,
a time to mourn and a time to dance,
5 a time to cast away stones and a time to gather stones together,
a time to embrace and a time to refrain from embracing,
6 a time to search and a time to count as lost,
a time to keep and a time to discard,
7 a time to tear and a time to mend,
a time to be silent and a time to speak,
8 a time to love and a time to hate,
a time for war and a time for peace.

Ecclesiastes 3

Where did anyone ever get the idea that the human condition is susceptible to sustained, unwavering happiness, joy, or even satisfaction? You are slightly more complex, intellectually and emotionally, than is an orangutan, dolphin, or elephant. By all appearances, *those* creatures are *less* susceptible to anxiety, depression and self-doubt than are members of your gibbering primate species. It may be that they enjoy a significant and underappreciated advantage. Perhaps there is some sense in which ignorance truly *is* bliss, insofar as those lacking the capacity for complex, abstract thought are, thereby, insulated from the most common sources of human psychiatric or psychological dysfunction. The human experience of depression and anxiety-related disorders is, to all appearances, unavailable to mammals with smaller brains that are, thus, not susceptible to massively complex psychological experiences. What dog ever fretted about the challenges of retirement? What bear ever worried that her cubs might be teased, bullied, or otherwise tormented by playfellows? What frog suffers from an imposter complex on the grounds that it sometimes catches flies by a lucky flick of its tongue? What squirrel ever felt sorry for itself on a cold winter's night? The big brain is not without its drawbacks. Do you feel sorry for yourself? *That* is shameful.

> 3 Join me in suffering, like a good soldier of Christ Jesus. 4 A
> soldier refrains from entangling himself in civilian affairs,
> in order to please the one who enlisted him. 5 Likewise, a
> competitor does not receive the crown unless he competes
> according to the rules. 6 The hardworking farmer should be
> the first to receive his share of the crops. 7 Consider what I am
> saying, for the Lord will give you insight into all things.
>
> 2 Timothy 2

What is this obsession with sports, games, competitive challenges, and with wins and losses, championships, and crushing defeats? *All* of this is *nothing*. It has no bearing whatsoever upon your moral purpose, the rectification of your character, or the accumulation of wisdom. You will be no better off as a reasoning creature no matter which team wins the Super Bowl. You will not incur vice if your nation's team fails to come home with an Olympic gold medal. What difference does it make who wears the gold, the silver, the bronze, who hoists the trophy, who gets to wear this or that belt for a while, etc.? Indeed, concern with games, combat matches, and athletic performance, *impedes* your progress in the general direction of wisdom and virtue. If you allow your equanimity to hinge upon the outcome of a fight, or the unfolding of the playoffs, then you treat your central mission as a trivial affair, subject to the contingencies of a game or a contest over which you have no control whatsoever. If a referee making a bad call in a football game can cause you to lose your equanimity, then your mind, and your emotions are *far* too fragile for the real world. When one of your loved ones dies unexpectedly, that referee and that game will not spring to the forefront of your consciousness. It is *nothing*. Do not get invested in bread and circuses. Are you so vapid and bereft of any sense of genuine purpose? A bunch of grown men play with a ball. That captures both your interest and your emotional allegiance?

What a shame. How, at your age, do you allow yourself to think and act as a child playing kickball? Pay attention to what is really at stake, and consider how little time remains. Leave games to children. Do not *play* at virtue. Grow up.

31But the men who had gone up with him replied, "We cannot go up against the people, for they are stronger than we are!"

32So they gave the Israelites a bad report about the land they
had spied out: "The land we explored devours its inhabitants,
and all the people we saw there are great in stature. 33We even
saw the Nephilim there—the descendants of Anak that come
from the Nephilim! We seemed like grasshoppers in our own
sight, and we must have seemed the same to them!"

Numbers 13

Tall people do not feel compelled to demonstrate their superior height as compared to shorter persons. That which is blindingly obvious need not be presented to an audience or explained *ad nauseam*. Anyone paying attention will not miss it. Yet *you*, on occasion, have found yourself showing off your allegedly superior intellect to those whom you regard as intellectually inferior, dimwitted, or cognitive cul-de-sacs of one type or another. What excuse can you produce for this behavior? If it requires special demonstration, perhaps your presumption of intellectual superiority is *no more than* presumptuousness. A giant need not make a show of the matter, or comment on his size. The truth is apparent to anyone with eyes. You, on the other hand, seek to demonstrate your mental agility, your rhetorical prowess (perhaps by using terms such as "rhetorical prowess"), and the fruits of your alleged higher education. This *reeks* of desperation. Is it anything other than insecurity that compels you to behave like a child pleading for Mommy's attention? Do you fear that the truth of *this* matter is *not* so obvious as is the case of the giant? Perhaps it is not. Perhaps you are just smart enough to understand how lacking you are by comparison with *genuine* intellectuals. Perhaps even *that* assessment is overly charitable. Maybe you are just another educated idiot. Try to be honest with yourself about this, and try not to irritate others with your pomposity. That is, to say the least, unbecoming (another overly charitable description). Insecurity is hardly a virtue. It is hardly a characteristic worthy of display. Stop waving your weakness over your head, as if it constitutes a proper object of admiration. Just stop.

29 At the appointed time he will invade the South again, but
this time will not be like the first. 30 Ships of Kittim will come
against him, and he will lose heart. Then he will turn back
and rage against the holy covenant and do damage. So he
will return and show favor to those who forsake the holy
covenant. 31 His forces will rise up and desecrate the temple
fortress. They will abolish the daily sacrifice and set up the
abomination of desolation.

32 With flattery he will corrupt those who violate the covenant,
but the people who know their God will firmly resist him.
33 Those with insight will instruct many, though for a time they
will fall by sword and flame or be captured or plundered.

Daniel 11

Depravity had to conceal itself from public view for most of human history. This was not exactly the worst state of affairs you could imagine. A world *without* depravity might have been preferable, but *that* world appears never to have been on offer. Today, you find degeneracy nearly everywhere you turn, proudly holding itself up to the citizenry, all but demanding obeisance from those who pass quickly by, seeking to avoid it. Wickedness insists upon drawing both attention and accolades to itself. This is an intensely peculiar inversion of values. When did decency and wholesomeness come to be regarded as quaint indications of parochialism and backwardness? When did the embrace of abomination, filth, and venality become markers of "sophistication"? Virgins and the sexually modest are shamed and held up as deformations of the human condition, while whores (of both sexes) and their pimps are celebrated. The corrupt are admired, while the humble and simple living are scorned, dismissed, and pitied. Faith is regarded as indicative of benightedness, whereas unreflective naturalism is the default position of "intellectuals." You hear and read that the material world is the *only* world, or the only world that matters, in any event. The *evidence* for this claim is simply *never* presented. What, after all, might such evidence look like? Perhaps the evidence is the "intellectual superiority" of the naturalists. Ah, well. Filth makes the world go round, it seems. This is cause for curiosity, perhaps, but not despair. The darkness has always been with us. It is just more easily visible, and more aggressively hectoring, than you might have expected. Of course, your expectations are *your* responsibility, are they not?

> 9The brother in humble circumstances should exult in his
> high position. 10But the one who is rich should exult in his
> low position, because he will pass away like a flower of the
> field. 11For the sun rises with scorching heat and withers the
> plant; its flower falls and its beauty is lost. So too, the rich
> man will fade away in the midst of his pursuits.
>
> 12Blessed is the man who perseveres under trial, because
> when he has stood the test, he will receive the crown of life
> that God has promised to those who love Him.
>
> James 1

This too shall pass away. All of "this" shall cease to be. *You* are going to die. Everyone that you have ever loved will meet the same fate. Your civilization will succumb to the pressures of history, challenges from within and without, and will go the way of all previous "empires." This entire planet, upon which all of humanity has hitherto played out the tragic farce of your species, will be incinerated when the sun goes supernova. Entropy will, ultimately, render this entire universe uninhabitable by any form of life whatsoever. The temperature of the future is in the neighborhood of absolute zero. The future is death. This fact is neither good nor bad, neither right nor wrong, neither a cause for joy nor a cause for weeping. What, after all, did you expect to follow after life in all of its various guises? Did you believe that, somewhere, a ceaseless celebration would spring into being? Perhaps it will. It is, however, unwise to allow your contentment to hinge upon finding that eternal festival. Do not *cling* to your life as it stands. Do not insist that the future *must* be this way or that. Do not *demand* a world that suits your reflexive whims. Who do you think you are? None of this is of your making. You are not in charge here. You are not even immortal. Do not tether your contentment to some unrealizable idealization that, even if once manifested, cannot last. Attempt to hold nothing fixed, apart from your central purpose, and your most fundamental values. Even these, of course, shall depart from this world at some point. You are not to allow them to disappear while you still draw breath, however. All else is a passing show. Do not be the dog that barks as the caravan is moving on.

15 All their evil appears at Gilgal,
for there I hated them.
I will drive them from My house
for the wickedness of their deeds.
I will no longer love them;
all their leaders are rebellious.
16 Ephraim is struck down;
their root is withered;
they cannot bear fruit.
Even if they bear children,
I will slay the darlings of their wombs.
17 My God will reject them
because they have not obeyed Him;
and they shall be wanderers
among the nations.

Hosea 9

You understand now that you are sentenced to live out your days in exile from the culture you once knew, and from the nation that you once believed you loved and revered. Perhaps emotional and psychological attachments of that type are unwise. Perhaps it is all just part of the detritus of childhood. It is, nonetheless, a bit irksome. Maybe it should not be, but it is. So it goes. It makes no difference where you go, or where you stay. You will *never* be at home in this world. Do *not* blame the world for this. This experience is nothing terrible. For a long time, you have understood your condition, but you have resisted embracing this facet of your nature, and of the world in which you find yourself embedded. Stop resisting. Stop denying who you are and what you are doing here. Diogenes was forced into exile, and he responded by sentencing those in his "homeland" to remain where they were—and *what* they were. Thus, his "revenge." Cain was sentenced to permanent exile, no matter where he might find himself. You are not better than either of them, are you? Indeed, a world that does not feel like home, also feels like a world in which you have no *desire* to feel at home, does it not? What is this place, what is *any* mere *place*, to you? Let your exile permeate your life. Embrace your homelessness. Be an itinerant observer who occasionally reports on and ridicules the passing scene. Now, put one foot in front of the other, and see where your feet take you next.

9 Now about brotherly love, you do not need anyone to write
to you, because you yourselves have been taught by God to
love one another. 10 And indeed, you are showing this love
to all the brothers throughout Macedonia. But we urge you,
brothers, to excel more and more 11 and to aspire to live quietly,
to attend to your own matters, and to work with your own
hands, as we instructed you. 12 Then you will behave properly
toward outsiders, without being dependent on anyone.

1 Thessalonians 4

There is a great deal to be said for solitude. You could hardly tolerate your fellow talking apes at all were it not for the frequent retreats into your mind, the privacy of your own consciousness, and the availability of physical separation from the company of others. How *do* they tolerate each other? Of all the rights about which persons clamor and argue, and about all of the liberties claimed with or without anything approaching rational justification, the right to be *left alone* is, perhaps, the most underappreciated. You are born into this world without your consent, and you have nothing to say about the early years, but you gradually develop the capacity to understand the reality in which you find yourself embedded well enough to know which components of the world are the ones from which you would like to dissociate yourself. The world hates to mind its own damned business, does it not? The world and the denizens thereof refuse to leave you alone. The world is a busybody, even though the vast majority of it does not know or care that you exist. Many persons are overly inquisitive (to put the matter diplomatically). This is no excuse for *you* to follow suit. To be left alone with one's thoughts, unaccompanied by the cacophony of ceaseless chatter, background noise, and staccato interjections of pointless commentary—this is worth fighting for, if need be. Your affinity for solitude need not meet with approval or even comprehension. What do you care what the world thinks of this tendency, or if it thinks of you *at all*? Let the rest of the world blather away. Freedom *from* association is a liberty worth defending. Find a space for calm contemplation. Do not waste this opportunity.

July

17 You say, "I am rich; I have grown wealthy and need nothing."
But you do not realize that you are wretched, pitiful, poor,
blind, and naked. 18 I counsel you to buy from Me gold refined
by fire so that you may become rich, white garments so
that you may be clothed and your shameful nakedness not
exposed, and salve to anoint your eyes so that you may see.
19 Those I love, I rebuke and discipline. Therefore be earnest
and repent.

20 Behold, I stand at the door and knock. If anyone hears My
voice and opens the door, I will come in and dine with him,
and he with Me. 21 To the one who is victorious, I will grant
the right to sit with Me on My throne, just as I overcame and
sat down with My Father on His throne.

Revelation 3

Indifference is the only rational attitude regarding conditions and events that lie outside the sphere of your direct control. This is a *rational* indifference, and not a knee-jerk dismissal of phenomena about which you experience sour grapes or feelings of resentment. Emotional and psychological attachments to conditions that can, and often will, turn out contrarily to your unreflective whims is an invitation to needless suffering. The outcome of an election should be nothing to you. Vote, or refrain from doing so, and concern yourself no further with the silly contest and its consequences. Nearly all of politics is for show, and very few politicians reveal their actual intentions and desires in public. Your colleagues are also none of your business, except insofar as you ought to control your behavior toward them. *Their* behavior is not your concern. Take note, pay attention, but do not allow any passionate attachments to develop. Has some material holding or other evaporated, declined in value, or been confiscated by some external power? Did someone deprive you of your toys? You had possessions that you possess no longer. So what? Understand that such holdings were never really *yours* in the first place. Elements of the material world are always on loan. You are to manage such matters as best you can, until the means of management are yours no longer. As for loved ones, you know the rule. Try your best. No one, however, is immortal.

17 Listen to me and I will inform you.
I will describe what I have seen,
18 what was declared by wise men
and was not concealed from their fathers,
19 to whom alone the land was given
when no foreigner passed among them:
20 A wicked man writhes in pain all his days;
only a few years are reserved for the ruthless.
21 Sounds of terror fill his ears;
in his prosperity the destroyer attacks him.
22 He despairs of his return from darkness;
he is marked for the sword.
23 He wanders about as food for vultures;
he knows the day of darkness is at hand.
24 Distress and anguish terrify him,
overwhelming him like a king poised to attack.
25 For he has stretched out his hand against God
and has vaunted himself against the Almighty,
26 rushing headlong at Him
with his thick, studded shield.

Job 15

Contemplate the "worst case scenario," and recognize that even the worst conceivable eventualities will, in one way or another, pass away and change into other conditions. No state of affairs is permanent. Change is the way of the world. Perhaps "the worst" culminates in your demise. Indeed, is there any "perhaps" about your demise? In a relatively short time, you will be dead, gone, and forgotten. What of it? Did you not know that your life is bound to culminate in your death? Have you not read about all of the historical figures that have "left the stage"? Are you not aware that most of your ancestors are unknown even to you, and forgotten by the rest of the population of this planet? The world has indefinitely many ways to kill you and conceal the fact that you ever existed. What is the difference if your death is the result of some kind of "disaster," or merely the termination of a slow process of dissipation and decline? Either way, you will be dead forever. Perhaps the "worst case scenario" leaves you alive for some time, and at the mercy of some malevolent force. Again, what of it? Did you not know that you live amid darkness and malefactors? Have you paid no attention to the history of your species and the many atrocities perpetrated thereby? You are not immune to torture and murder. Anything can happen. Your travails will *not* last forever. They will, however, last (merely) until you die. So... take comfort.

7So now, this is what the LORD God of Hosts, the God of Israel,
says: Why are you doing such great harm to yourselves? You
are cutting off from Judah man and woman, child and infant,
leaving yourselves without a remnant, 8provoking Me to
anger by the work of your hands, burning incense to other
gods in the land of Egypt where you have gone to reside.

As a result, you will be cut off and become an object of cursing
and reproach among all the nations of the earth. 9Have you
forgotten the wickedness of your fathers and of the kings of
Judah and their wives, as well as the wickedness that you and
your wives committed in the land of Judah and the streets of
Jerusalem? 10To this day they have not humbled themselves
or shown reverence, nor have they followed My instruction
or the statutes that I set before you and your fathers.

Jeremiah 44

How have you gotten this far without the intervention of the fraud police? Surely, they are going to knock on your door, take you away, and reveal all of your inadequacies any day now. You know that you have nothing of value to offer anyone, and you know where this story ends. Of course, all human stories end in the same place, do they not? As for all of those who have gone before you, and those yet to come, what are *you* to them? Those who have "changed the world," and those who are to change it further in the future—they shall not change human nature one whit. No one will eradicate stupidity, corruption, or hubris. Humanity is stubbornly incorrigible and consistently resistant to most cures and purgatives. Jesus "changed the world," or so you are told. There are, of course, a lot of people who call themselves "Christians." Apart from that, people mostly seem to be as disastrous and self-absorbed as ever. Alexander the Great conquered much of the world that was known to him. As a result, those areas he conquered... still make war, and still produce generation after generation of stupid, talking apes. People make war with more effective weapons than in Alexander's day. The efficiency of mass slaughter has improved markedly. The armies massed against each other speak in different tongues these days. Is this a form of "progress"? Perhaps. *L'chaim*! To life!

7Submit yourselves, then, to God. Resist the devil, and he will
flee from you. 8Draw near to God, and He will draw near
to you. Cleanse your hands, you sinners, and purify your
hearts, you double-minded. 9Grieve, mourn, and weep. Turn
your laughter to mourning, and your joy to gloom. 10Humble
yourselves before the Lord, and He will exalt you.

11Brothers, do not slander one another. Anyone who speaks
against his brother or judges him speaks against the Law and
judges it. And if you judge the Law, you are not a practitioner
of the Law, but a judge of it. 12There is only one Lawgiver and
Judge, the One who is able to save and destroy. But who are
you to judge your neighbor?

James 4

It is time to discard all the superfluous trappings, possessions, concerns, interests, and all other wastes of your time and energy. Indeed, it is long past time for you to "put away childish things," is it not? You cannot be confident that you have a great deal of life still lying before you. No one can be confident of the future. Perhaps another decade or two will lapse before you do, or perhaps you will drop dead before the clock strikes twelve tonight. Consider all of the friends, family, and associates who did not live to the age you will be if you should make it to your next birthday. Do not be presumptuous. Who promised you a future? Where is "tomorrow" written into your contract with Fate? Do not allow your life to be wasted on the expectation that there will be ever more opportunities to improve, and limitless access to the tools of reason and fortitude. That is a fool's wager. An aneurism, a stroke, Alzheimer's disease, or any one of countless causes can take a mind functioning within normal parameters from you at any moment. There may be no warning whatsoever. The world will probably last for a very long time to come. *You* will be present for virtually *none* of it. By contrast with the billions of years past, and those yet to be, your life is not even the blink of an eye. *You* are not even a speck in the blinking eye. Your life is less than a rumor passed along among a group of fast-perishing primates. The sky grows dim. The time is *now*. What do you think you are doing?

5 Then the LORD came down to see the city and the tower
that the sons of men were building. 6 And the LORD said, "If
they have begun to do this as one people speaking the same
language, then nothing they devise will be beyond them.
7 Come, let Us go down and confuse their language, so that
they will not understand one another's speech."

8 So the LORD scattered them from there over the face of all
the earth, and they stopped building the city. 9 That is why
it is called Babel, for there the LORD confused the language
of the whole world, and from that place the LORD scattered
them over the face of all the earth.

Genesis 11

Do not dally with the wrong tribes, and do not pretend that you cannot tell which tribes are yours, which are compatible with yours, and which are utterly at odds with everything that you have ever valued. There is no good excuse for *hating* members of other tribes, and there is no good reason to wish them any harm, but do not pretend that everyone can or should coexist in the same area with people who want nothing to do with them. No one believes that we are "all equal," all compatible, or that all cultures are equally worthy of esteem and respect. This bizarre bit of dogma has done more than its share of damage to the fabric of the only tribe with which you have ever experienced even the slightest hint of kinship. The fiction of mutually compatible equality across all persons and all cultures is nothing short of poison, and will, almost certainly, prove fatal to at least one of the antagonists in the inevitable conflict. It *is* coming. Indeed, the conflict in question is already raging. Skirmishes have been going on for some time now. You would prefer an amicable separation, and a rational method of leaving each other undisturbed. This possibility is, of course, not on offer. In fact, the mere *recognition* and acknowledgement of indissoluble differences is not to be had. Many of the "powers that be" refuse to admit that the conflict exists, and actively work to punish anyone who points out the obvious. It is not clear where to turn. It is not always clear which people are "yours." You may be a tribe of *one*. Even if there are others like you, they are unlikely to seek your company. Can you blame them? Solitude remains available to you... for now.

1So the king and Haman went to dine with Esther the queen,
2and as they drank their wine on the second day, the king
asked once more, "Queen Esther, what is your petition? It
will be given to you. What is your request? Even up to half
the kingdom, it will be fulfilled."

3Then Queen Esther replied, "If I have found favor in your
sight, O king, and if it pleases the king, grant me my life as
my petition, and the lives of my people as my request. 4For
my people and I have been sold out to destruction, death, and
annihilation. If we had merely been sold as menservants and
maidservants, I would have held my peace, because no such
distress would justify burdening the king."

5Then King Xerxes spoke up and asked Queen Esther, "Who is
this, and where is the one who would devise such a scheme?"

6Esther replied, "The adversary and enemy is this wicked
man—Haman!"

And Haman stood in terror before the king and queen.

Esther 7

Do not allow yourself to be stymied by uncertainty about potential public response to your behavior, your work, or your utterances. If you have done your level best to explore the facts, analyze the available data, and arrive at a reasoned conclusion, then act upon the information at your disposal in the most efficient and felicitous fashion you are able. If what you say or do in this manner upsets friends, family, colleagues, or the public at large, so be it. If everyone ignores whatever you have to say, which seems quite likely and not at all illegitimate, then know that you have done what you could, and that what you could manage amounted to, more or less, nothing as far as everyone else is concerned. Accept the consequences, whatever they may be, with the grace of a rational adult. If disapprobation is your lot, let it be so. If it turns out that you are shouting into a void that is fine as well. What do you need with anyone's approval? Children concern themselves with such matters. You are not permitted to conduct yourself in the manner of a child. If you meet with approval, this is equally insignificant. What do you care for the hoots and applause of a colony of talking simians? Find a branch overlooking the others, and pay attention.

29 At the appointed time he will invade the South again, but
this time will not be like the first. 30 Ships of Kittim will come
against him, and he will lose heart. Then he will turn back
and rage against the holy covenant and do damage. So he
will return and show favor to those who forsake the holy
covenant. 31 His forces will rise up and desecrate the temple
fortress. They will abolish the daily sacrifice and set up the
abomination of desolation.

32 With flattery he will corrupt those who violate the covenant,
but the people who know their God will firmly resist him.
33 Those with insight will instruct many, though for a time they
will fall by sword and flame or be captured or plundered.

34 Now when they fall, they will be granted a little help, but
many will join them insincerely. 35 Some of the wise will fall,
so that they may be refined, purified, and made spotless until
the time of the end, for it will still come at the appointed time.

Daniel 11

Someone "let you down" today. Someone behaved in a way that conflicted with your beliefs and expectations. Whose fault is that? The expectations are *yours*, are they not? Control your expectations like a rational adult. If your beliefs do not conform to reality as it unfolds, it is not reality that deserves blame or disapprobation. Your beliefs ought to be constrained by the world as you perceive it, and by reason. Someone broke your trust. *You* placed your trust in a person who proved to be unworthy of that trust, did you not? Thus, your misjudgment is the origin of your disappointment. Furthermore, you allowed another person's conduct to surprise you, and to disappoint you. Have you not lived among your fellow human beings long enough to anticipate this type of behavior? Are you so weak, emotionally, that the sounds and motions of another person's body, mouth, and mind can cause you distress? How pathetic. Failures, foibles, stupidity, and corruption are hardly novel. A moral failure shocks you? Know thyself. Corruption is a surprise? Know thyself. Watching the corrupt receive rewards and accolades for their malfeasance is like watching objects fall when dropped, or watching people get wet when it rains. Get over your indignation. Grow up, simpleton. The world is, more or less, as it has always been. You have changed nothing.

$_{13}$Enter through the narrow gate. For wide is the gate and
broad is the way that leads to destruction, and many enter
through it. $_{14}$But small is the gate and narrow the way that
leads to life, and only a few find it.

$_{15}$Beware of false prophets. They come to you in sheep's
clothing, but inwardly they are ravenous wolves. $_{16}$By their
fruit you will recognize them. Are grapes gathered from
thornbushes, or figs from thistles? $_{17}$Likewise, every good
tree bears good fruit, but a bad tree bears bad fruit. $_{18}$A good
tree cannot bear bad fruit, and a bad tree cannot bear good
fruit. $_{19}$Every tree that does not bear good fruit is cut down
and thrown into the fire. $_{20}$So then, by their fruit you will
recognize them.

Matthew 7

There are many, *many* ways for you and your life to go horribly wrong. The path to virtue is narrow, mostly uphill, and littered with stumbling blocks. This is no reason to allow your feet to tread any other path. Indeed, any other path will lead you nowhere worth going, and all the other paths are overcrowded already. The masses are enamored with the paths that lead, supposedly, to fame, or to fortune, or to excess, or through various forms of self-abasement en route to some unworthy goal or other. Foolish pursuits are legion, and their devotees are as numberless as the stars in the sky. What would cause you to want to count yourself among that pathetic, numberless number? The path of the imbecile is easy to tread, but each step along it is as pointless and self-defeating as the next. Surely, you aim for something higher and nobler than the life of the average simpleton. Then again, maybe you are no better, no braver, and no more worthy of the good life than those whom you despise and disdain. Perhaps you have become what you have beheld all these years.

If so, yours is a sad, pathetic, and richly deserved lot. You *will* become what you make of yourself and, unfortunately, you *are* what you have made of yourself thus far. So, what do you intend to become? Get about the business before you. Keep your nose to the grindstone, and walk the path that those whom you admire have travelled. *Stray* from that path, and suffer what you have, thereby, earned.

20 The perverse in heart are an abomination to the LORD,
but the blameless in their walk are His delight.

21 Be assured that the wicked will not go unpunished,
but the offspring of the righteous will escape.

22 Like a gold ring in a pig's snout
is a beautiful woman who lacks discretion.

23 The desire of the righteous leads only to good,
but the hope of the wicked brings wrath.

Proverbs 11

You find yourself walking among the undead, and you wonder if you are not gradually, or perhaps not so gradually, becoming one of them. Is there, or is there not, a bit of the zombie within you? What, after all, distinguishes you from the hollow-eyed, vacant, lumbering masses of humanity trudging through their days, and medicating themselves so as to survive the nights and insulate themselves from the terror of thoughts experienced in the absence of some form of external stimulus or other? They are horrified at the prospect of being left alone with nothing but their own thoughts to occupy them. What else is boredom, after all, but a form of discontent with oneself and the contents of one's own mind? Perhaps something frightens you as it rattles around the confines of your private consciousness. Maybe you are afraid of yourself. Maybe everyone is similarly afraid. What on earth are any of you doing? What is supposed to be the point of the many games, the insipid posturing, and the ceaseless pursuit of iterated pleasures—each of which provides declining utility? There can be only so many hedonic peaks to be surmounted before the subsequent downslope proves unendurable. You pursue nothing in particular, and you judge those whom you encounter in the same pointless pursuits. If this is the best that you can manage, you may as well find a trough of slop and end the pretense of loftier hopes.

11When I was a child, I talked like a child, I thought like a
child, I reasoned like a child. When I became a man, I set
aside childish ways. 12Now we see but a dim reflection as in
a mirror; then we shall see face to face. Now I know in part;
then I shall know fully, even as I am fully known.

1 Corinthians 13

Disappointment is evidence of ignorance, stupidity, or psychological and emotional weakness. To "suffer disappointment" is to admit irrationality or ignorance. You have lived in this world long enough to know the way of things. What, after all, could the complaint possibly be? Is your career not going as well as you had hoped? Perhaps it provides less by way of fulfillment than you had expected. The elements of your career that are up to you and determined by your efforts can only disappoint you if *you* have failed in some fashion or other. You chose this method of sustaining yourself. You have opted to pursue your career in the manner, in the places, and among the colleagues that you have experienced. You have chosen this. As for those aspects of your career that are *not* up to you, it is simply foolish to allow your emotional states to depend upon those facets of the project. Does "your" culture let you down in some manner or other? Were you expecting better? If so, you are thinking and behaving as a child. Where did you get the idea that you have any control over the evolution and development of the massively complex and unruly beast that you think of, infelicitously, as "your" culture? Only a child believes that any one person can control such matters. It is much the same with anything else that you might identify as a "disappointment." Can you control it? Do so, or admit that you are a failure. Can you *not* control it? If so, put aside all concern with it. Desist in the cognitive framing that lends itself to disenchantment. You have no business being "enchanted" in the first place. Put away childish, irrational desires. Do not insist that the world must satisfy your fantasies.

16 Their infants will be dashed to pieces
before their eyes,
their houses will be looted,
and their wives will be ravished.
17 Behold, I will stir up against them the Medes,
who have no regard for silver
and no desire for gold.
18 Their bows will dash young men to pieces;
they will have no mercy on the fruit of the womb;
they will not look with pity on the children.
19 And Babylon, the jewel of the kingdoms,
the glory of the pride of the Chaldeans,
will be overthrown by God
like Sodom and Gomorrah.

Isaiah 13

Do not hesitate to resort to violence in self-defense or, more importantly, in defense of innocents in your care and under your protection. Consider the loss to be incurred if you fail to act at the crucial moment. It is not the loss to you, with which you ought to be concerned, but rather the loss of life, limb, or peace of mind that will be visited upon those victimized due to your failure. Never rely on the presumption of humanity or decency when your mind or your gut tell you that a threat confronts family, community, or innocent persons who are unable to defend themselves. It is very unwise to "hope for the best," and wait to see if "the best" manifests instead of the less palatable alternatives. Constant vigilance is required. You are not permitted to let your guard down, or to allow your attention to flag when the situation is less than safe. Beware crowds, dark places, and strangers approaching with no apparent justification. Avoid rash overreaction, and quickly assess all available information. Do not, yourself, become a threat to innocents. Once the danger threshold is crossed, however, there is to be no second-guessing, and no restraint until the threat is eliminated. Do what you must. Strike as if your child's life depends upon it. Mercy is not properly reserved for those who would harm you or yours.

18 Servants, submit yourselves to your masters with all respect,
not only to those who are good and gentle, but even to those
who are unreasonable. 19 For if anyone endures the pain of
unjust suffering because he is conscious of God, this is to be
commended. 20 How is it to your credit if you are beaten for
doing wrong and you endure it? But if you suffer for doing
good and you endure it, this is commendable before God.

1 Peter 2

You sometimes wonder why a virtuous God would allow so much suffering to afflict his beloved "children." You have, on occasion, wavered in your faith because of this conundrum. This is childishness. You know precisely nothing of God's designs or intentions. Indeed, you do not know, and cannot express an opinion with any real confidence, about God's existence. In other words, you do not even know if it is rational to believe in God... but you *do* believe, do you not? So, why would God allow you, and every person who has ever lived before you, as well as every person occupying the planet at the moment, to suffer physically, emotionally, psychologically, and in every other manner that besets your species—to say nothing of all the suffering imposed upon nonhumans now, and throughout history? Consider this resolution. You simply do not know, and will probably never understand why it is so. Is this not the message conveyed in the Book of Job from the Hebrew Bible? Is this not precisely what a rational adult ought to expect? People suffer. How, exactly, is this an argument that God does not exist? Perhaps He has His reasons. Perhaps He does not need reasons. Perhaps He is just a phantasm conjured by children in desperate need of an infallible father figure. Perhaps... you have *no* idea. Settle down, you primate with an overly unctuous imagination. Why should you understand such matters? Be grateful that you exist at all. That is enough. That is *more* than enough. You are not fit to complain about the conditions of your existence. Gratitude. That is exactly enough.

10 Therefore this is what the Lord GOD says: "Since it became
great in height and set its top among the clouds, and it grew
proud on account of its height, 11 I handed it over to the
ruler of the nations, for him to deal with it according to its
wickedness. I have banished it.

12 Foreigners, the most ruthless of the nations, cut it down and
left it. Its branches have fallen on the mountains and in every
valley; its boughs lay broken in all the earth's ravines. And
all the peoples of the earth left its shade and abandoned it."

Ezekiel 31

Petty despotism among persons in government positions, or institutional bureaucracies, has reached pandemic proportions. Surely, this fact cannot possibly surprise you. Lord Acton told us that "power corrupts," and this applies to trivial, incidental authority as much as it applies to "absolute power." There is something about authority that entails a temptation to its misuse. There is something seductive about commanding other persons. Perhaps there is something about human beings that causes most of them to be incapable of resisting such temptations, and perhaps it is not power, in and of itself, that is problematic. It may be that humanity is perverse to its very core, and it may be that authority is simply an opportunity to express this core perversity more explicitly than is normally the case. Persons holding power, however, is a condition so frequently and so relentlessly used for malign purposes, that you should be at least vaguely suspicious of those who seek it, and you should be *very* suspicious of those who are willing to spend enormous amounts of time, money, and energy in the pursuit of power. In other words, *never* trust a politician. Furthermore, do not entrust *yourself* with power over other people. Monitor your intentions any time you are authorized to wield authority over anyone other than yourself. You are at least as susceptible to corruption as is anyone else. Do not pretend that you are not part of the problem.

27 Zion will be redeemed with justice,
her repentant ones with righteousness.
28 But rebels and sinners will together be shattered,
and those who forsake the LORD will perish.
29 Surely you will be ashamed of the sacred oaks
in which you have delighted;
you will be embarrassed by the gardens
that you have chosen.

30 For you will become like an oak whose leaves are withered,
like a garden without water.
31 The strong man will become tinder
and his work will be a spark;
both will burn together,
with no one to quench the flames.

Isaiah 1

Savagery is not without its merits. That may seem counterintuitive, but you have had more than one occasion to resort to it and, in retrospect, not all of those resorts to savagery were unjustified. Defense of self, home, family, and decency may require bursts of brutality unvarnished with sentiment, hesitation, or even a hint of civility. An armed intruder bursting through the door of your home, where your children sleep, is not to be met with gentle chastisement, criticism of his character, or restrained indignation. The intruder is to be met with closed fists, weapons, and ruthlessly efficient violence designed to incapacitate immediately and in a fashion from which quick recovery is impossible. Indeed, a failure to respond to a clear and present danger to your children is nothing short of despicable cowardice. If the intruder has to be put down like a sick animal, then you are obligated to euthanize the threat. Your family is not properly placed at risk in a misguided effort to maintain civility. You will protect your family with every measure at your disposal, and every fiber of sinew you can marshal to their defense, or you will die an ignominious failure.

1And God spoke all these words:

2"I am the LORD your God, who brought you out of the land of Egypt, out of the house of slavery.

3You shall have no other gods before Me."

Exodus 20

If millions of Israelites did *not*, in fact, hear the Lord speak at Sinai, how exactly was that story fabricated, marketed, and sold to generations of Jews who believed, in overwhelming numbers, that their ancestors heard the Lord's voice at the foot of that mountain? The question is sincere. How was that story not met with incredulity and dismissiveness the first time it was presented to a Jewish audience? Why was the response not something along the lines of, "Why did our parents and grandparents never tell us this story, and how did *you* learn of this miraculous event that was, somehow, concealed from the rest of us?" Would *you* believe someone who told you that all of your ancestors experienced a miraculous event, but that this event had been entirely extirpated from memory before it was transmitted to those ancestors who preceded you by a few generations? Who lost the story, how was it concealed from you, and who recovered evidence of the event sufficient to compel your belief in the truth of the story? No... really. If the Sinai revelation, allegedly witnessed by millions of Israelites, did not actually happen, how did anyone convince Orthodox Jewry that it did? This is a puzzle. The *national* revelation, the *mass* revelation, is not easily explained away. If God did not speak to a gathering of millions of people, then the world is bereft indeed. Humanity is alone, adrift, and there is little cause for any overarching hope. If, on the other hand, the story of the mass revelation in *Exodus* is true, then you ought to learn how to appreciate the miracle that is your presence in the world God made.

August

5 His people have acted corruptly toward Him;
their spot is not that of His children,
but of a perverse and crooked generation.
6 Is this how you repay the LORD,
O foolish and senseless people?
Is He not your Father and Creator?
Has He not made you and established you?

Deuteronomy 32

You live in an anthropic universe. This is not easily explained. Even if there are an infinite number of universes, or an infinite expanse of *this* universe, it simply does not follow that "everything that *can* happen, will happen," or that *any* universe or *any* section of this universe will be habitable by the complex, intelligent life you find on this planet. There could have been an infinite number of universes, each of which contained nothing more than a finite number of subatomic particles that never assembled so much as a single atom, or one stable molecule. The constants that govern the behavior of matter, energy, the development of space and time, etc., appear to fall within excruciatingly narrow and fairly rigidly bounded ranges that are necessary for an anthropic environment to emerge anywhere. The odds against humanity evolving out of the "primordial stew" are nothing short of staggering. The term "astronomical" seems particularly apt in this context, does it not? Perhaps the universe looks as if it is designed for intelligent life because it *is* designed for intelligent life. You *cannot*, of course, know this with anything approaching certainty. Indeed, there are any number of alternative, purely naturalistic explanations, most of which are probably well beyond your understanding. The inference to intelligent design is, however, not particularly indefensible. Maybe God made the world, and it may be that *you* are part of the plan. Is this possibility not worth a pause and a bit of reflection?

13They presented false witnesses who said, "This man never
stops speaking against this holy place and against the Law.
14For we have heard him say that Jesus of Nazareth will
destroy this place and change the customs that Moses handed
down to us."

15All who were sitting in the Sanhedrin looked intently at
Stephen, and they saw that his face was like the face of an
angel.

Acts 6

Heretics and dissidents are not to be underestimated or dismissed out of hand. Their beliefs arise, presumably, in something like the same manner that beliefs pop into anyone else's head. Upon inspection and analysis, many persons turn out to be poorly informed, dishonest, or charlatans of one form or another. Others are speaking gibberish. This cannot, however, be said of all those who voice criticisms of prevailing orthodoxies. Not all dissidents are wrong, and not all heretics are worthy of condemnation or dismissal. Consider the contributions, whether they are, all things considered, positive, negative, or neutral, of Copernicus, Galileo, Luther, Erasmus, Calvin, Kant, and Nietzsche. Others who declined to accept politely the constructs that they encountered have had their attitudes shaped by these dissident thinkers, and much of our contemporary worldview, including various facets of our understanding of the human condition, are, at the very least, partially produced by a bit of challenge and resistance against formerly prevailing worldviews. What contribution can *you* claim to have made that warrants even the most vague comparison with Copernicus? When did you stand against the received power, authority, and influence of a massive enterprise that looked to be invincible? You have mostly "gone along" and you have mostly gone unnoticed. This is not without justification. You are mostly unworthy of notice, are you not? What impact have you had on our understanding of the world and of our place in it? Perhaps your life will prove to be an epiphenomenon passing without any impact whatsoever. Let it be so. You are still obligated to live the best life that you can.

> 24 Do you not know that in a race all the runners run, but
> only one receives the prize? Run in such a way as to take
> the prize. 25 Everyone who competes in the games trains with
> strict discipline. They do it for a crown that is perishable, but
> we do it for a crown that is imperishable. 26 Therefore I do not
> run aimlessly; I do not fight like I am beating the air. 27 No, I
> discipline my body and make it my slave, so that after I have
> preached to others, I myself will not be disqualified.
>
> 1 Corinthians 9

Games of chance are tolerable as long as they do not interfere with your central purpose, or undermine the material well-being of your family. Gambling away money or resources that deprive your loved ones of security, or of valuable opportunities, is a shameful indulgence. Either indulge not at all, or do so in very restricted moderation, and stick to games that are not *entirely* a matter of chance, but that also involve some level of skill, strategy, or the exertion of intellectual or physical energy. Intellectually slothful gambling is one of the least admirable wastes of time and money. Most card games require the deployment of skills pertaining to mathematics and probability assessment. Slot machines, however, are strictly for lazy imbeciles. If you want to witness human devolution, just hang out at a casino and watch idiots shoving cash into one-armed bandits as if they are compelled to fritter away any dignity they may once have possessed. You may wager, in a reasonable fashion, on games such as Scrabble®, or Blackjack, Poker, Backgammon, and contests involving crossword puzzles, or arm-wrestling. Keep the wagers *well* within your means, and be careful to avoid emotional or psychological entanglements, such as despair at a loss, or exuberance at a win. The winning and losing is not entirely up to you. Only your participation and the quality of your performance are within *your* control. Do not participate is such contests when you are feeling muddleheaded from lack of sleep, or when your mood might lend itself to anger or frustration. Brief diversions of this type are tolerable. Do *not* make them a way of life.

> 1 Do not judge, or you will be judged. 2 For with the same
> judgment you pronounce, you will be judged; and with the
> measure you use, it will be measured to you.
> 3 Why do you look at the speck in your brother's eye, but fail
> to notice the beam in your own eye? 4 How can you say to
> your brother, "Let me take the speck out of your eye," while
> there is still a beam in your own eye? 5 You hypocrite! First
> take the beam out of your own eye, and then you will see
> clearly to remove the speck from your brother's eye.
> 6 Do not give dogs what is holy; do not throw your pearls
> before swine. If you do, they may trample them under their
> feet, and then turn and tear you to pieces.
>
> Matthew 7

Waste no further time attempting to reason with those who have demonstrated contempt for reason and the pursuit of wisdom. Conversations or debates with the dim or the dishonest are exercises in perverse futility. Such persons are of no value to you and are unworthy of your concern. All attempts to help them are doomed to failure, resources spent on their interests are like stepladders constructed for the benefit of jellyfish. Do not be deluded about attempts to assist those to whom help is either unwelcome or valueless. *You* may, indeed, find some use for the ladder, but the jellyfish will not and cannot. A clam can do nothing with a calculator. Never embrace childish platitudes about "equality" or the "brotherhood of all humanity." You have seen far too much of humanity to believe that all are intrinsically equal in any sense whatsoever, and you have had more than enough experience with your fellow talking apes to want any more of them "in your family" than is dictated by fairly narrowly defined biological entanglements. Anyone more genetically distant than a first cousin, at the outermost connection of biology and marriage, is no "family" with which you need to be intimately concerned. Foolish strangers and indigestible cultures are particularly unwelcome at "family reunions." Take care of *your own*. Leave the rest to other "families."

1Then I saw a new heaven and a new earth, for the first heaven
and earth had passed away, and the sea was no more. 2I saw
the holy city, the new Jerusalem, coming down out of heaven
from God, prepared as a bride adorned for her husband.

Revelation 21

Do not fret about life after death, the world to come, resurrection, reincarnation, heaven, hell, purgatory, or any of the other post-mortem possibilities suggested by scripture, wisdom traditions, or superstition. Live this life as well, as reasonably, and as virtuously as you can manage. Do your best to be upstanding and honorable. If there is something after this "vale of tears," then a life of decency should be sufficient to secure a palatable version of the possibilities allegedly on "the other side." Sustained decency *might* just get you to heaven. If, on the other hand, there is no life, no experience, no continuing consciousness beyond this terrestrial sphere, then you have exactly as much reason to try your best to become as wise, as virtuous, as decent, and as upstanding as you would have if the road to heaven lay open before you. Do not be good for the sake of gaining paradise. Do not pursue wisdom and virtue for the sake of applause, accolades, or the approval of other persons. That is shallow, cynical, and self-serving "virtue." Indeed, there is nothing especially virtuous about pursuing narrow, material self-interest. If there *is* a God, He will see through the ruse, and your ersatz efforts will be for naught. Why would the Lord reward selfish egoism? As for the opinions of other persons, since when was the pursuit of public approbation listed among the admirable endeavors? If there is *not* a God, you owe it to yourself, and to those who depend upon you, to live the most fulfilling and flourishing life you can. You will find it difficult to be a decent parent, spouse, or citizen if you do not even manage to live the life of a decent, honorable human being. What is flourishing without wisdom and virtue? Leave the pursuit of pleasure to pigs, children, and celebrities.

7 Were you the first man ever born?
Were you brought forth before the hills?
8 Do you listen in on God's council
or limit wisdom to yourself?
9 What do you know that we do not?
What do you understand that is not clear to us?
10 Both the gray-haired and the aged are on our side—
men much older than your father.
11 Are the consolations of God not enough for you,
even words spoken gently to you?
12 Why has your heart carried you away,
and why do your eyes flash,
13 as you turn your spirit against God
and pour such words out of your mouth?

Job 15

What is there to be said about your ignorance that is not blindingly obvious to nearly everyone you encounter? What, exactly, *do* you know? You hope that there is a God, but you can be no more confident that this hope maps onto reality than the atheist can be confident in the contrary mapping. You believe that you have a sense of what virtue and decency require of you, but it is possible that you are mistaken about the proper goals, the general moral principles, or the applicable decision procedures and methods of attaining virtue. Perhaps the nihilists are correct, and all concern with good and evil is misguided or meaningless. You think that you have, for the most part, a fairly accurate grasp of the physical world and the laws that govern it, but the quantum underpinnings of the world you experience are utterly opaque to you and, for all you know, the laws of nature are subject to change or nullification a nanosecond from now. You believe that the sun will rise tomorrow because it has risen for all of your yesterdays and today, but you are also fairly confident that tomorrow's sunrise is promised to no one, and the world as you "know" it will, at some point, cease to be. Consider all that you do not know, and humble yourself accordingly. Drop your arrogant pretension to authority. You know *nothing*.

13 Yet You concealed these things in Your heart,
and I know that this was in Your mind:
14 If I sinned, You would take note,
and would not acquit me of my iniquity.
15 If I am guilty, woe to me!
And even if I am righteous, I cannot lift my head.
I am full of shame
and aware of my affliction.
16 Should I hold my head high,
You would hunt me like a lion,
and again display Your power against me.
17 You produce new witnesses against me
and multiply Your anger toward me.
Hardships assault me
in wave after wave.

Job 10

You occupy a spinning glob of mud revolving around a nondescript star, hurtling through one galaxy among untold billions of others. On the other hand, you breathe in and out, and you think thoughts about this world, your place in it, and about your own insignificance. Is this something like a paradox? If you are a conscious being, endowed with the capacity to reason (on occasion), then perhaps you are not quite *as* insignificant as an inanimate asteroid that does nothing other than obey the laws of physics. Then again, what do you do that is not obedient to the same laws? It is not at all clear how neurological complexity or self-awareness liberates you from the laws of nature and its vast web of causes and effects. Does your brain do anything other than respond to the dictates of your heredity and environment (broadly construed)? Are you so arrogant as to believe that you initiate events *ex nihilo*—like some god unencumbered by flesh, bones, gravity, and worldly constraints? You should hope to avoid that kind of hubris. You are a bag of self-conscious meat. This is not denigration, but merely description.

1My son, if you have put up security for your neighbor,
if you have struck hands in pledge with a stranger,
2if you have been trapped by the words of your lips,
ensnared by the words of your mouth,
3then do this, my son, to free yourself,
for you have fallen into your neighbor's hands:
Go, humble yourself,
and press your plea with your neighbor.
4Allow no sleep to your eyes
or slumber to your eyelids.
5Free yourself, like a gazelle from the hand of the hunter,
like a bird from the fowler's snare.

Proverbs 6

Patience is, in many cases, a virtue. Indeed, there are many instances in which patience is the only viable option. Throwing a fit and screaming do not readily facilitate the project of helping a toddler learn to walk. In other instances, however, patience is counterproductive or worse. When time is of the essence, it is unwise to wait patiently while people die, a nefarious plot unfolds, or damages continue to increase to persons or property. Responding patiently to, for example, an infestation of your home by termites is likely to result in pervasive, possibly irreversible and, almost certainly, very expensive, needless deterioration of structural integrity. It is not always so different with the health, well-being, or integrity of persons, communities, or nation states. It is unwise to respond with patience if a loved one expresses an intention to commit a heinous crime, an act of suicide, or a pointlessly dangerous feat of stupidity. If possible, intervene immediately, effectively, and in a manner that undercuts the problematic intention quite thoroughly. Restraining a child running toward traffic, for example, is not properly undertaken in a patient or circumspect manner. Grab the kid! Do not let go until you are quite certain the imminent danger has passed. Some threats are properly met with urgency. Some threats are properly addressed as if lives hang in the balance. When you recognize this type of threat, leap into action and do not desist until the threat is eradicated.

1 You shall not spread a false report. Do not join the wicked by
being a malicious witness.
2 You shall not follow a crowd in wrongdoing. When you
testify in a lawsuit, do not pervert justice by siding with a
crowd. 3 And do not show favoritism to a poor man in his
lawsuit.

Exodus 23

There is all too much disingenuous "outrage," today, and it is all too frequently met with insincere apology and contrition. This bizarre Kabuki dance plays out on an almost daily basis in the media, and even among your friends, family, and colleagues. Intellectual laziness is somewhere near the heart of this phenomenon. People who lack the capacity to construct an argument in support of their position, and people who are simply too slothful to exert the intellectual effort required to conduct careful critical analysis, seem to be the only gleeful participants in this type of charade. Those who shriek, "Racism!" or "Sexism!" or some other fashionable shibboleth of the day do so as if the utterance itself is evidence of guilt in the matter. Unfortunately, this behavior is mostly tolerated, or even embraced as if it is virtuous, and this response is almost entirely a matter of cowardice. False accusations should incur the same consequences, the same penalties, as would be imposed upon those actually found guilty of the charge in question. If actual bigotry would incur termination from one's employment, a false charge of bigotry should incur a proportional punishment. Do not bear false witness, or participate in dishonest allegations. Do not allow yourself to become a coward or a liar.

16 But they and our fathers became arrogant and stiff-necked
and did not obey Your commandments.
17 They refused to listen and failed to remember
the wonders You performed among them.
They stiffened their necks and appointed a leader
to return them to their bondage.
But You are a forgiving God,
gracious and compassionate,
slow to anger and rich in loving devotion,
and You did not forsake them.

18 Even after they had cast for themselves
an image of a calf and said,
"This is your God who brought you up out of Egypt,"
and they had committed terrible blasphemies...

Nehemiah 9

Does anyone gain as much wisdom from success as from failure? Failure is, in most cases, the more effective teacher across a wide range of experiences, but you shrink from it, deny it, and marinate in worry at the potential that you may experience failure. Is this not irrational? Consider the most important and most valuable lessons you have ever learned. Many of them required failure and all of the attendant consequences. Would you be willing to forgo the lessons learned, merely so that you might also have averted the failure that preceded it? If so, you must not truly value wisdom or progress. Any failure that is not fatal or permanently debilitating to yourself or others is nothing at which you ought to boggle, or before which you ought to cower. Go forth, fail for all you are worth, and learn as much as you can from the experience. Do not fail on purpose, as this is both paradoxical and, arguably, perverse. Always try your best. When, however, your best simply is not good enough, do not hang your head or avert your eyes. Absorb. Learn. Improve.

5 A fool rejects his father's discipline,
but whoever heeds correction is prudent.

6 The house of the righteous has great treasure,
but the income of the wicked is trouble.

7 The lips of the wise spread knowledge,
but not so the hearts of fools.

8 The sacrifice of the wicked is detestable to the LORD,
but the prayer of the upright is His delight.

Proverbs 15

Do not begrudge anyone any of their possessions or positions of power or authority. In all probability, the possessions and power are more trouble than they are worth, and the possessor is certainly not wiser, more virtuous, or more intellectually fulfilled for having them. Do not conflate wealth with moral health, and do not confuse power with earned authority. If you seek a flourishing life, do not cast an envious eye upon those who overflow with money, material trappings, and many subordinates subject to their command. Let them have the headaches, ulcers, and sleepless nights that attend their "status." Leave them to their delusions of grandeur. Always remember to value wisdom and decency more than anything for which they may be traded away—foolishly. Celebrity is not a proper pursuit, wealth usually costs far more than it is worth, and political power typically leads to corruption and needless conflict. What do you want with *any* of it? Which of your heroes was wealthy and powerful? Emulate those worthy of your admiration, and eschew concern for all that they disdained.

17 And to Adam He said:

"Because you have listened to the voice of your wife
and have eaten of the tree
from which I commanded you not to eat,
cursed is the ground because of you;
through toil you will eat of it
all the days of your life.
18 Both thorns and thistles it will yield you,
and you will eat the plants of the field.
19 By the sweat of your brow
you will eat your bread,
until you return to the ground—
because out of it were you taken.
For dust you are,
and to dust you shall return."

20 And Adam named his wife Eve, because she would become the mother of all the living.

Genesis 3

Remind yourself, as often as is necessary, that your life will not, in the grand scheme of things, last very long. This is not morbid, this is not "dark," this is not an exercise in self-flagellation; rather this is essential for staying focused on your central purpose and maintaining a sense of moral urgency. At any moment, your journey on this planet might end. Consider how much time you have had, and how much of it you have wasted on pointless pursuits. Is it wise to allow yourself to waste even more time? Surely, you cannot take pride in profligacy or prodigality. Why, then, do you persist in behaviors in which you can take no pride? Your time grows shorter with each passing moment. The Emperor compelled a subject to remind him, frequently, "Remember, thou art mortal." This is a wise practice for a "commoner" such as yourself, as well as it is for a man who rules an empire. You need not hire a subordinate to follow you around, reminding you of your mortality. This duty is best not left to another person's discretion. *You* take responsibility.

1 This is the oracle that Habakkuk the prophet received in a vision:

2 How long, O LORD, must I call for help
but You do not hear,
or cry out to You, "Violence!"
but You do not save?
3 Why do You make me see iniquity?
Why do You tolerate wrongdoing?
Destruction and violence are before me.
Strife is ongoing, and conflict abounds.
4 Therefore the law is paralyzed,
and justice never goes forth.
For the wicked hem in the righteous;
therefore, justice is perverted.

Habakkuk 1

How many people destroy their lives by making the same mistake over and over again? If you allow yourself to become one of those people, know that you will deserve the consequences that are bound to ensue. Indeed, it would be something of a shame if you were to avoid dire consequences that you richly deserve. You will learn *nothing* if you are not caused to suffer when you have behaved in a manner that typically entails and justifies suffering. Imagine surviving, entirely unscathed, an automobile accident, for which you are entirely responsible, that kills a whole family of innocent victims. Could you live with yourself in the absence of suffering for your malfeasance? Could you live with yourself after such an event under *any* circumstances? Never seek to avoid punishment. Even if you are innocent, embrace any punishment that your fellow talking apes, or nature, or the world at large imposes upon you. Do not complain about the injustice. Do not complain at all. Have you *never* avoided a punishment that you richly deserved? Do you recall complaining about *that* injustice? Do not expect injustice to occur only to your *benefit*. This is petulance.

> 10 Then he told me, "Do not seal up the words of prophecy
> in this book, because the time is near. 11 Let the unrighteous
> continue to be unrighteous, and the vile continue to be vile;
> let the righteous continue to practice righteousness, and the
> holy continue to be holy."
>
> 12 "Behold, I am coming quickly, and My reward is with Me,
> to give to each one according to what he has done. 13 I am the
> Alpha and the Omega, the First and the Last, the Beginning
> and the End."
>
> Revelation 22

There *are* terrible people in the world. Do not kid yourself about this. Perhaps none of them are entirely beyond redemption, but they are certainly beyond redemption due to *your* efforts. It is nothing short of perverse to expect decency from those who have repeatedly demonstrated that they have no interest in decency, virtue, or good and evil. All of us are imperfect. Of this, you have never had a doubt. Do not, however, conflate pervasive imperfection with acute malevolence. The genocidal maniac is not morally equivalent to people who cheat a bit on their taxes. The child rapist will not be reformed or redeemed, and will not become a trustworthy babysitter. The tax cheat is not nearly so far removed from decency and the hope of rehabilitation, as is the mass murderer. There are degrees of evil. There is a moral continuum. Do not kid yourself that you occupy the same region as the Saints, but make absolutely certain that you never drift toward the opposite end of that sliding scale. As for those who have lived their entire lives around the margins of the evil end of the continuum, do not turn your back on them for an instant. You are obligated to be more responsible and more rational than to allow the wicked into your life, your family, or your circle of friends. Do *not* associate with filth.

11 For this is what the LORD spoke to me with a strong hand, instructing me not to walk in the way of this people:

12 "Do not call conspiracy
everything these people regard as conspiracy.
Do not fear what they fear;
do not live in dread.
13 The LORD of Hosts is the One
to regard as holy.
Only He should be feared;
only He should be dreaded,
14 and He will be a sanctuary."

Isaiah 8

Learn to extend moments of peace, serenity, and equanimity. Direct your will at persisting in the wholesome feeling of calm, and learn to remain imperturbable for longer and longer periods of time. Much as you exercise your body to maintain physical fitness, you must exercise your power of cognitive control, and your strength of will to maintain psychological and emotional fitness. Only in this way can you hope to withstand the inevitable slings and arrows of Fate, the unavoidable challenges to your peace of mind, and the inveterate temptation to collapse under the weight of a world that remains stubbornly indifferent to your well-being. Death, indeed, *will* take you, but do not let it find you weeping in a corner, or curled up in the fetal position bemoaning your lot. Let death find you in a condition of rational self-possession. Let death find you smiling. Let death find you staring it in the face and daring it to do its worst. Let death fear *you*. Perhaps this last injunction cannot be fulfilled, perhaps death is without fear, but setting an unattainable goal does not preclude progress in the direction that goal demands.

September

20 So they watched Him closely and sent spies who pretended
to be sincere. They were hoping to catch Him in His words
in order to hand Him over to the rule and authority of the
governor. 21 "Teacher," they inquired, "we know that You
speak and teach correctly. You show no partiality, but teach
the way of God in accordance with the truth. 22 Is it lawful for
us to pay taxes to Caesar or not?"

23 But Jesus saw through their duplicity and said to them,
24 "Show Me a denarius. Whose image and inscription are on
it?"

"Caesar's," they answered.

25 So Jesus told them, "Give to Caesar what is Caesar's, and to
God what is God's."

26 And they were unable to trap Him in His words before the
people; and amazed at His answer, they fell silent.

Luke 20

How many times have you regretted speaking? There are many, many more such instances than there are occasions on which you have regretted *not* speaking, are there not? It seems that speaking has caused you far more suffering and difficulty than has simply keeping your big mouth shut. Have you learned nothing from this? This obnoxious habit of running your mouth and saying things that no one wants or needs to hear would appear to be both irrational and deleterious to both your interests and your character. When was the last time that anyone expressed gratitude for the opportunity to listen to you blather on about anything? When was the last time that you were impressed by the "wisdom" popping out of your stupid face? Try to maintain dignified silence unless and until you are fairly confident that you are in a position to make a valuable contribution. Also, try not to become overly confident too easily where this matter is concerned. If you have nothing to say that is informative, useful, comforting, or inspirational, try to remember that you have the right to remain silent. It is not merely a good idea—there is actually a *law*.

29 When Joseph looked up and saw his brother Benjamin, his
own mother's son, he asked, "Is this your youngest brother,
the one you told me about?" Then he declared, "May God be
gracious to you, my son."

30 Joseph hurried out because he was moved to tears for his
brother, and he went to a private room to weep. 31 Then he
washed his face and came back out. Regaining his composure,
he said, "Serve the meal."

Genesis 43

Pay no attention whatsoever to the private lives or personal peccadilloes of people you encounter, read about, hear about, etc. None of this is any of your business, none of it has anything to do with acquiring virtue or wisdom, and all of it serves to do nothing but distract you from legitimate purposes and projects. Is there insufficient work lying before you? Have you ample time to spare? If not, do not waste time and energy on insignificant, prurient interests or morbid, lurid curiosities. A busybody is hardly worthy of your emulation, and you have been annoyed often enough by people who cannot seem to mind their own business, that you certainly ought to know better than to follow their example. The Golden Rule is applicable here, as it is in so many other instances. If you do not want people prying into the areas of your life that you regard as private and personal, then you certainly have no business prying into their lives in this objectionable manner, nor do you have any business encouraging others to do so, passing along foolish gossip, or facilitating loose talk. Grow up and pay attention to the project of improving *yourself*. Other people have flaws, but theirs are no worse than yours, and ought to be none of your concern.

12 Whoever shows contempt for his neighbor lacks judgment,
but a man of understanding holds his peace.

13 A gossip reveals a secret,
but a trustworthy person keeps a confidence.

14 For lack of guidance, a nation falls,
but with many counselors comes deliverance.

Proverbs 11

If you *ever* behave in untrustworthy fashion, you are *never* entitled to expect or demand anyone's trust thereafter. Even if you correct this flaw and become a pristinely trustworthy person, you cannot fault those who decline to place their trust in you, given that you have violated someone's trust at any point in the past. Their distrust is not unfair. You will have earned it. Be grateful, indeed, if *anyone* ever places their faith in you again. Virtue and decency are *not* playthings to be taken up when convenient and laid aside when it suits your whims. Do *not* toy with vice and insist that the dalliance *must* be forgiven. You have neither the power nor the moral authority to make any demands whatsoever upon another person's beliefs, attitudes, or expectations. Perhaps *you* might be inclined to forgive and forget trivial slights or misbehaviors from the distant past, but your assessment of such matters cannot be imposed upon others, and you are a fool if you insist that anyone else *must* adopt your perspective. Forgiveness is, in many instances, a virtue. Insistence upon *forcing* this virtue upon others, however, is clearly a *vice*. Mind your business.

14Is Israel a slave?
Was he born into slavery?
Why then has he become prey?
15The young lions have roared at him;
they have growled with a loud voice.
They have laid waste his land;
his cities lie in ruins, without inhabitants.
16The men of Memphis and Tahpanhes
have shaved the crown of your head.
17Have you not brought this on yourself
by forsaking the LORD your God
when He led you in the way?

Jeremiah 2

Entrust *nothing* of any importance to a fool or a liar. Your family is not to be toyed with or placed at risk for the sake of appeasing *anyone,* and certainly not for the sake of maintaining conviviality with moral or intellectual defectives. If adopting a civil posture with persons of that stripe introduces even the slightest danger to any member of your family, jettison civility and do not lapse into it again with persons of low character. Do not be gentle in this area. Let there be no uncertainty in your behaviors, your utterances, or your demeanor. Send the utterly unambiguous message that dangerous foolishness and deleterious dishonesty will be met with any and all force you can muster to the contrary; be crystal clear that there is no upper limit to the measures you are willing to take in defense of your loved ones. Communicate with certainty that you are willing to do absolutely anything necessary to destroy the threat with which you are confronted. Let this not be insincere. Do not run the risk of presenting a sham deterrent. What must be done, you *must* do. Even lions should fear to approach you when you stand in defense of your family.

> 1On the twenty-fourth day of the same month, the Israelites
> gathered together, fasting and wearing sackcloth, with dust on
> their heads. 2Those of Israelite descent separated themselves
> from all the foreigners, and they stood and confessed their
> sins and the iniquities of their fathers.
>
> 3While they stood in their places, they read from the Book
> of the Law of the LORD their God for a quarter of the day,
> and they spent another quarter of the day in confession and
> worship of the LORD their God.
>
> Nehemiah 9

Accept responsibility for all flaws attributed to you, rightly or wrongly, fairly or unfairly, and offer neither excuses nor defenses. If the allegations are erroneous, then someone has formed a false belief about you, or made a false claim. What is that to you? Do you have control over what anyone else believes, whether those beliefs pertain to you or not? You need not defend yourself, outside of a court of law—and, indeed, you have no *legal* obligation to defend yourself even in *that* context (though mounting a defense against false allegations in court may be morally and practically necessary to sustain those who depend upon you). Making *excuses* in the face of false allegations is perverse and dishonest. Perverse dishonesty simply cannot be noble, and it should never be regarded as a viable option. Do not even consider such an option. If, on the other hand, the allegations are accurate, then you ought to be grateful for the instruction and for having this character flaw brought to your attention. Do not underestimate the value of attentive detractors. Sometimes, other people perceive flaws in your character that would otherwise remain undetected through your own introspection and self-observation. Do not offer a defense of the indefensible, and make no excuse for it either. Set about eradicating the defect. *That* is your principal concern.

1 The words of the Teacher, the son of David, king in Jerusalem:

2 "Futility of futilities,"
says the Teacher,
"futility of futilities!
Everything is futile!"

3 What does a man gain from all his labor,
at which he toils under the sun?

Ecclesiastes 1

Your vanity was on display again today, was it not? Where does this impulse to show off come from, and how do you continue to fall prey to the childish need for attention? Indeed, you cannot have advanced far beyond the perspective and the understanding of a small child, if you still behave as if garnering attention from others is worth your time and effort. Like a five-year-old yelling, "Look at me! Look at me!" you reek of desperation, and you debase yourself by feeding off of the approval of the crowd, or the applause of persons whom you do not even regard as equals, or as worthy of *your* respect. How pathetic is that? How emotionally weak you must be to seek plaudits from persons you do not even esteem. Putting aside the intrinsic quality of the crowd and individual components of it, you cannot seriously believe that you ennoble yourself, that you find higher ground, that you make progress in the direction of wisdom and virtue, by putting on a show to please others. What other people think of you, what they believe about you, is simply none of your business, and it ought to remain well outside the sphere of your concern. Stop behaving like a small child in a terrible school play. Can you not lay vanity aside and conduct yourself as an adult?

5 Her foes have become her masters;
her enemies are at ease.
For the LORD has brought her grief
because of her many transgressions.
Her children have gone away
as captives before the enemy.

6 All the splendor has departed
from the Daughter of Zion.
Her princes are like deer
that find no pasture;
they lack the strength to flee
in the face of the hunter.

7 In the days of her affliction and wandering
Jerusalem remembers all the treasures
that were hers in days of old.
When her people fell into the hand of the adversary,
she had no one to help.
Her enemies looked at her,
laughing at her downfall.

Lamentations 1

The coalition of the weak, the pathetic, the cowards, the liars, and the corrupt has taken up the reins of power in your culture, and they are bent on directing the masses to Sodom or over the nearest, highest cliff. Their depravity is insufficient to satisfy them. It is not enough that they make their way to the bottom, but they regard it as absolutely essential that they drag the entire civilization all the way to Hell with them. The deviant is never happy simply being a deviant in solitude. The deviant loves company far more than misery has ever loved it. The coward is affronted by the presence of the courageous, the liar hates everyone who tells the truth, the weak detest and resent the strong, and every pathetic, malformed creature desires that destruction of anyone and anything that is beautiful, flourishing, healthy, or noble and admirable. A tipping point approaches. Indeed, you may have to look over your shoulder, at this point, to see when that point was surpassed. This is not the first time in history that humankind teetered on the brink of self-immolation, but it may well be the last. Should you be more troubled by the whiff of doom in the air? Is civilization still worth saving? That the answer is less than clear—this constitutes something tragic in and of itself.

15 "How can you say, 'I love you,'" she told him, "when
your heart is not with me? This is the third time you have
mocked me and failed to reveal to me the source of your great
strength!"

16 Finally, after she had pressed him daily with her words and
pleaded until he was sick to death, 17 he told her all that was
in his heart: "My hair has never been cut, because I have been
a Nazirite to God from my mother's womb. If I am shaved,
my strength will leave me, and I will become as weak as any
other man."

Judges 16

Most days you do *not* find yourself longing for the sweet, warm embrace of death or the peace and serenity of the tomb. Every so often, however, you find that you vaguely envy the dead. You ponder, wistfully, getting shut of this world and, far more importantly, of its moronic, disgusting inhabitants. Generally, this condition passes fairly quickly. Generally, you regard such spells, in retrospect, as silly departures from rationality, or perhaps a mere consequence of indigestion or an insufficient night's sleep. On other, much more rare occasions, you wonder if your retrospection is not infected with a little bit of rationalization. You *do* die at the end, after all. The universe *is* unimaginably vast, and your life really *does* constitute an infinitesimal quantity of time and space. Interacting with people, especially large numbers of people, actually *is* enervating and largely pointless. *They* all die at the end *also*. The human race *will* become extinct, the universe *will* become uninhabitable, and the entropy goes on *ad infinitum*. Of course, you *did* have liver for lunch today. Perhaps it does not agree with you.

5 Showing partiality to the wicked is not good,
nor is depriving the innocent of justice.

6 A fool's lips bring strife,
and his mouth invites a beating.

7 A fool's mouth is his ruin,
and his lips are a snare to his soul.

8 A gossip's words are like choice morsels,
and they sink into the inmost being.

Proverbs 18

There *are* people who deserve a beating. This may be an *uncomfortable* truth, but that does not make it any less true. Indeed, some such persons seem incapable of learning via any method that does *not* involve some form of violence. Fortunately, for such persons, the world always, eventually, lays a beating on *everyone*. No one gets out alive; no one gets out unscathed, and no one ever gains mastery over nature, the laws that govern it, or the management of more than a sliver of the matter and energy that comprise the natural world. This is *not* tragic. The effort to avoid suffering imposed by the natural world is often misguided. The attempt to *control* nature is *always* misguided. Anyone who attempts to tread where "the gods" have forbidden them access, thereby invites disaster. There is no hedonic paradise devoid of suffering. If there *were* such a realm, you would do well to avoid it. Utopianism is childish. Building a "perfect society" is a quixotic endeavor, and it is, and always will be, doomed to abject failure. Your flaws are not unique. They are to be found among the masses, and they will always afflict any collection of persons, irrespective of any method of governance or the absence of governance. Suffer what you must. Do not complain. Do not attempt to escape. Learn.

20 Then Absalom said to Ahithophel, "Give me counsel. What should we do?"

21 Ahithophel replied, "Sleep with your father's concubines whom he has left to keep the palace. When all Israel hears that you have become a stench to your father, then the hands of all who are with you will be strengthened."

22 So they pitched a tent for Absalom on the roof, and he slept with his father's concubines in the sight of all Israel.

23 Now in those days the advice of Ahithophel was like the consultation of the word of God. Such was the regard that both David and Absalom had for Ahithophel's advice.

2 Samuel 16

Avoid giving unsolicited advice. Your temptation to offer advice that no one has requested is unhealthy, unwise, and it manifests in obnoxious interpersonal interactions without which the world could readily and happily make do. Who are *you*, after all, to pose as an oracle? If your advice is not requested, you probably ought to avoid offering it. There is precisely *nothing* about you and *no* accomplishments attributable to *you* that would warrant this bizarre presumption that you are entitled to offer an opinion about what anyone else should do. You really ought to direct your attention at your own foibles, and you really ought to exert your efforts where they might do some good, and desist in yapping at people who never asked for your input. Get to work on improving yourself, and stop being an irritating busybody. Do you not have enough of your own inadequacies on which to bend your will? Are you not sufficiently disastrous to attract your own helpful attention? The next time you feel that inclination to advise someone who has requested no advice, punch yourself in the face instead. *That* might accomplish something.

> 28When the men heard this, they were enraged and began
> shouting, "Great is Artemis of the Ephesians!" 29Soon the
> whole city was in disarray. They rushed together into the
> theatre, dragging with them Gaius and Aristarchus, Paul's
> traveling companions from Macedonia.
>
> 30Paul wanted to go before the assembly, but the disciples
> would not allow him. 31Even some of Paul's friends who were
> officials of the province of Asia sent word to him, begging
> him not to venture into the theatre.
>
> Acts 19

There is nothing admirable about developing convivial relations with individuals or collections of persons who are, clearly, less than admirable. How much effort should you put into the project of "getting along" with miscreants, dimwits, or sloths? Furthermore, you place your own character at risk through association of *any* kind with disreputable louts. There is nothing to be gained through companionship among the morally and intellectually bereft. This strange expectation to the contrary, promulgated through media, education, and institutions, that we must find "common ground" with each other, or that we ought to compromise in order to avoid conflict, is simpleminded, platitudinous nonsense. There are many, *many* people with whom you should *never* compromise. If you find yourself becoming friendly with idiots and liars, you should become less friendly. It is better to live in isolation than to keep company with people who will do nothing but corrode your character and lead you into filthy behavior. Pollution comes in many forms. Pay at least as much attention to the company you keep, as you do to the food you eat, the drink you imbibe, and the air you breathe. Cancer can be personified. Avoid carcinogens.

13So you were adorned with gold and silver, and your clothes
were of fine linen, silk, and embroidered cloth. You ate fine
flour, honey, and oil. You became very beautiful and rose to
be a queen. 14Your fame spread among the nations on account
of your beauty, for it was perfect in the splendor I bestowed
on you, declares the Lord GOD.

15But because of your fame, you trusted in your beauty and
played the harlot. You lavished your favors on everyone who
passed by, and your beauty was theirs for the asking. 16You
took some of your garments and made colorful high places for
yourself, and on them you prostituted yourself. Such things
should not have happened; never should they have occurred!

Ezekiel 16

Physical beauty is wildly overrated, almost entirely useless for any practical purposes, and it has caused more trouble, more foolishness, and more conflict than could possibly be warranted. This fascination with appearances should be a source of embarrassment, and everyone who succumbs to temptations associated with the pull of physical attraction should be distrusted in all matters pertaining to judgment or discrimination. If you ever place any value in a person's attractiveness, including your own, you have, thereby, exposed your stupidity, your immaturity, and you have earned a weakened character. Socrates was regarded as the most ugly man in all of Athens. Do you, therefore, respect him less than you would have had he been an Adonis? Certainly not! Does a beautiful adulteress command your respect? Of course not! Never allow a "halo effect" to alter your assessment of any person, from any walk of life, on any occasion. Beautiful people are not, thereby, better people. Character, intellect, and behavior are proper objects of approval or disapprobation. Physical appearance is *nothing*. Beware pretty poison.

[26]Therefore these days are called Purim, from the word Pur.

Because of all the instructions in this letter, and because of all
they had seen and experienced, [27]the Jews bound themselves
to establish the custom that they and their descendants and
all who join them should not fail to celebrate these two
days at the appointed time each and every year, according
to their regulation. [28]These days should be remembered and
celebrated by every generation, family, province, and city,
so that these days of Purim should not fail to be observed
among the Jews, nor should the memory of them fade from
their descendants.

[29]So Queen Esther daughter of Abihail, along with Mordecai
the Jew, wrote with full authority to confirm this second letter
concerning Purim. [30]And Mordecai sent letters with words of
peace and truth to all the Jews in the 127 provinces of the
kingdom of Xerxes, [31]in order to confirm these days of Purim
at their appointed time, just as Mordecai the Jew and Queen
Esther had established them and had committed themselves
and their descendants to the times of fasting and lamentation.

Esther 9

A labor of love is, at least in most cases, a noble and admirable endeavor. Working long hours, simply for the sake of maximizing remuneration, or becoming a workaholic in order to avoid other aspects of your life, is simplemindedness, at the very least, and, quite possibly, a symptom of some underlying neurosis. A spouse and parent, working eighty hours a week, may be doing an exemplary job of providing for the material well-being and security of the family, but may not be doing quite such an exemplary job of *being* a parent or spouse. A wife who is pleased that her husband spends *that* much time working is probably not particularly enamored of the man she married. Similarly, a husband who *wants* his wife devoting that much time and attention to matters other than her family, probably experiences a marriage that is *far* less than ideal. As for the children, if they like Mommy and Daddy maximizing time and energy applied to making money, and ignoring household affairs, something unwholesome is sure to attend that preference. Do not fall in *love* with a job or career. There are *people* whom you can and should love. Do not undervalue those people. Do not be a wealthy fool.

4 This is the account of the heavens and the earth when they
were created, in the day that the LORD God made them.

5 Now no shrub of the field had yet appeared on the earth,
nor had any plant of the field sprouted; for the LORD God
had not yet sent rain upon the earth, and there was no man
to cultivate the ground. 6 But springs welled up from the earth
and watered the whole surface of the ground.

7 Then the LORD God formed man from the dust of the ground
and breathed the breath of life into his nostrils, and the man
became a living being.

8 And the LORD God planted a garden in Eden, in the east,
where He placed the man He had formed. 9 Out of the ground
the LORD God gave growth to every tree that is pleasing to
the eye and good for food. And in the middle of the garden
were the tree of life and the tree of the knowledge of good
and evil.

Genesis 2

Health is not to be taken for granted, and you must remain cognizant of the fact that your body can fail at literally *any* moment. You can be laid low by an aneurism before you take your next breath. Your heart can stop beating while you sleep tonight. Every step that you take could be your last. None of this is cause for concern. These are ineradicable elements of the human condition. You never earned birth in human form. Regarding your life with anything other than gratitude is peevish and irrational. Every moment that you enjoy a *healthy*, physically flourishing human life, you should be ashamed to utter a single word of complaint, even in the confines of your own consciousness, about *anything* at all. Breathe in and out, note that your body can breathe, you live on a planet with an atmosphere that allows creatures like you to exist on it (for a while), and marvel at the wondrous complexity both inside and outside of your body, that allows you to keep breathing in and out (for a while). If you cannot appreciate this moment of your life, perhaps it is time to consider an alternative.

> 25 “There will be signs in the sun and moon and stars, and
> on the earth dismay among the nations, bewildered by the
> roaring of the sea and the surging of the waves. 26 Men will
> faint from fear and anxiety over what is coming upon the
> earth, for the powers of the heavens will be shaken. 27 At that
> time they will see the Son of Man coming in a cloud with
> power and great glory. 28 When these things begin to happen,
> stand up and lift up your heads, because your redemption is
> drawing near.”
>
> Luke 21

Social constructs and customs may be necessary evils, but you ought to remember that they are *evils* nonetheless. Every time you adhere to some expectation that you regard as irrational, remind yourself that you have indulged in a moment of surrender and submission. Checking to see if your clothes “match” (whatever that means) is tantamount to obeying the dictates of some unknown mob, and doing so for the sole purpose of avoiding criticism concerning an “issue” that you regard as utterly insignificant. What do you care about *fashion*? It is like agreeing to put your left foot on the floor *first* each morning, before you place your right foot on the floor, because you agreed that a coin toss would determine this procedure for the rest of your life. Suppose you agreed, for the sake of conviviality, that heads would mean right foot first, and tails would mean left foot first, for the rest of your life. Consider what a stupid and pointless agreement that would be. How stupid is the handshake as a ritual of greeting? You keep doing it, though. You do it because it is generally expected, and criticism or disapproval will ensue if you refrain from doing it. Perhaps someone may be offended. Have you *nothing* better with which to concern yourself? Idiocy.

October

10 Luxury is unseemly for a fool—
how much worse for a slave to rule over princes!

11 A man's insight gives him patience,
and his virtue is to overlook an offense.

12 A king's rage is like the roar of a lion,
but his favor is like dew on the grass.

13 A foolish son is his father's ruin,
and a quarrelsome wife is like a constant dripping.

14 Houses and wealth are inherited from fathers,
but a prudent wife is from the LORD.

Proverbs 19

Spoken words are nothing more than sounds, written words are nothing more than ink or pixels in patterns, and neither sounds nor patterns have any power over you with which you do not endow them. If *you* allow anger to arise within you because someone utters sounds, then you, thereby, damage your own psyche and your own character. Do not blame the speaker for your irrational, immature reaction to the utterance. If you allow irrationality to befoul your mood because someone types pixels onto a computer screen, then you, thereby, afflict your own mind. Do not attribute your condition to the author of the patterned pixels. You are, in *every* such case, to blame *yourself* for any and all suffering that you impose upon yourself due to a lapse in self-discipline, insufficient mental conditioning, or a dearth or rational indifference to matters beyond your control. How dare you blame the external world for your inadequacy? Take responsibility for your weakness. Reinforce the citadel of reason within you. Otherwise, resign yourself to anger, frustration, and discontent.

> 8 If you see the oppression of the poor and the denial of justice
> and righteousness in the province, do not be astonished at the
> matter; for one official is watched by a superior, and higher
> still are over them. 9 The produce of the earth is taken by all;
> the king himself profits from the fields.
>
> 10 He who loves money is never satisfied by money, and he
> who loves wealth is never satisfied by income. This too is
> futile. 11 When good things increase, so do those who consume
> them; what then is the profit to the owner, except to behold
> them with his eyes?
>
> 12 The sleep of the worker is sweet, whether he eats little or
> much, but the abundance of the rich man permits him no
> sleep.
>
> 13 There is a grievous evil I have seen under the sun: wealth
> hoarded to the harm of its owner, 14 or wealth lost in a bad
> venture, so that when he has a son there is nothing to pass on.
>
> 15 As a man came from his mother's womb, so he will depart
> again: naked as he arrived. He takes nothing for his labor to
> carry in his hands. 16 This too is a grievous evil: Exactly as a
> man is born, so he will depart. What does he gain as he toils
> for the wind? 17 Moreover, all his days he eats in darkness,
> with much sorrow, sickness, and anger.
>
> Ecclesiastes 5

How exactly could an "afterlife" or life after death possibly work? What form could you take after your body has expired? Perhaps there is a disembodied, nonphysical consciousness or an immaterial soul. If this is the case, how does it experience anything without eyes to see, ears to hear, etc.? Some claim that the soul can see and hear. If that is the case, why are there blind and deaf people? What is it about embodiment that prevents the eyes and ears "of the soul" from functioning? Perhaps you will be resurrected, in bodily form, and you will see, hear, and feel in much the same way that you do now. Presumably, this new body will not age, become decrepit, break down, or cause the type of suffering to which your current body subjects you. Otherwise, an eternal post-mortem persistence in bodily form would have to be construed as a punishment or, at the very least, a horrible misfortune. An eternal physical decline is nothing for which you ought to hope. Perhaps there is a God and He made only *this* world. What, then, of justice and virtue. This world is not much for justice or mercy, is it? Does this challenge your faith? Is it merely a puzzle? Is it both? Perhaps.

6Furthermore, the LORD said to Moses, "Put your hand inside
your cloak." So he put his hand inside his cloak, and when he
took it out, his hand was leprous, white as snow.

7"Put your hand back inside your cloak," said the LORD.

So Moses put his hand back inside his cloak, and when he took it out, it was restored, like the rest of his skin.

8And the LORD said, "If they refuse to believe you or heed
the witness of the first sign, they may believe that of the
second. 9But if they do not believe even these two signs or
listen to your voice, take some water from the Nile and pour
it on the dry ground. Then the water you take from the Nile
will become blood on the ground."

Exodus 4

Do persons who lack faith envy the faithful? Few if any would admit as much, but this is hardly proof that they decline to admit it though it is true. This is, of course, not proof of the contrary either. There would be something strange, would there not, if the faithless did not, at least on occasion, envy the faithful? Surely, faith provides comfort and hope to at least some of the faithful, at least some of the time. From the fact that a belief is comforting, it does not follow that the belief in question is true. Comforting untruths are legion. The comfort, itself, however, is intrinsically pleasing, and some degree of envy must derive from the faithless lacking the unique form of comfort that is only to be gleaned from faith in the Almighty. Even if the faithful are a bunch of superstitious rubes, there may be genuine benefits to be derived from the superstition. Suppose you are faced with the choice of adopting a comforting belief for which you lack compelling evidence, or declining to adopt that comforting belief for which compelling evidence is lacking. Can reason dictate the adoption of a worldview that renders life hopeless? It could. The big brain that enables you to conceive of God also produces conundrums of this type. One of God's little jokes, perhaps.

> [1]Now when Solomon had finished building the house of the
> LORD and the royal palace, and had achieved all that he had
> desired to do, [2]the LORD appeared to him a second time, as
> He had appeared to him at Gibeon. [3]And the LORD said to
> him,
>
> "I have heard your prayer and petition before Me. I have consecrated this temple you have built by putting My Name there forever; My eyes and My heart will be there for all time.
>
> [4]And as for you, if you walk before Me as your father David
> walked, with a heart of integrity and uprightness, doing all
> I have commanded you, and if you keep My statutes and
> ordinances, [5]then I will establish your royal throne over Israel
> forever, as I promised your father David when I said, 'You
> will never fail to have a man on the throne of Israel.'"
>
> 1 Kings 9

Learn to value, learn to pursue, and learn to maintain *simplicity*. This pertains to your values, your material holdings, your life path, and your interpersonal interactions. Needless complexity plagues the contemporary world. Perhaps it has always been so, or always seemed so, but you live *now*, and what has always been or always seemed to be does not confront you at the moment. You are confronted with more choices, more possibilities, and more potential resources than ancient peoples could have imagined. This does not entail, as some seem to imagine, that life is *better* today than in the ancient world. Life may well be better today, in many respects, than it was in ancient Greece, Rome, or China. People generally live longer, and palliative measures to deal with pain are more readily available and more effective than ever before, and technology is clearly superior, *vastly* superior, to anything that people "enjoyed" in centuries past. There are, however, detriments that attend these advances. Finding silence, finding peace in nature, and finding simplicity within your daily life is, arguably, more difficult today than ever before. Keep your concerns as simple as possible. The alternative is simply bewildering.

13For You formed my inmost being;
You knit me together in my mother's womb.
14I will praise You,
for I am fearfully and wonderfully made.
Marvelous are Your works,
and I know this very well.
15My frame was not hidden from You
when I was made in secret,
when I was woven together
in the depths of the earth.
16Your eyes saw my unformed body;
all my days were written in Your book
and ordained for me
before one of them came to be.

Psalm 139

Dostoyevsky's Grand Inquisitor is not at all pleased at the Savior's return. The Messiah is *unwelcome*. Indeed, the Inquisitor desires to burn this threat to Christendom at the stake. Do you believe that he is alone among those who call themselves "Christians"? Surely not! This is, of course, no critique of Christianity or even of Christians, but only the recognition that human beings are often *terrified* by the prospect of getting what they claim to desire. It is one thing to form an idealization and to long for its fruition, but it is another thing entirely to experience that for which you have longed, or for which you believed that you have longed. A wish granted could become the imposition of a curse that you place upon yourself. How many have desired freedom from their circumstances, only to find that the very freedom for which they had hoped becomes, once realized, terrifying and burdensome. If you could only escape this place, this job, this system, this oppressor, or this guilt—then you could live the life you have been hitherto denied. Really? Will you not carry all of your inadequacies with you into this "new life" of yours. Grow up. Your greatest problem is, and shall remain, *you*.

7 Ask and it will be given to you; seek and you will find; knock
and the door will be opened to you. 8 For everyone who asks
receives; he who seeks finds; and to him who knocks, the
door will be opened.
9 Which of you, if his son asks for bread, will give him a stone?
10 Or if he asks for a fish, will give him a snake? 11 So if you who
are evil know how to give good gifts to your children, how
much more will your Father in heaven give good things to
those who ask Him!
12 In everything, then, do to others as you would have them
do to you. For this is the essence of the Law and the prophets.
13 Enter through the narrow gate. For wide is the gate and
broad is the way that leads to destruction, and many enter
through it. 14 But small is the gate and narrow the way that
leads to life, and only a few find it.

Matthew 7

If you could peer into the mind of every person you meet, would you have more respect for them, less respect, or would you retreat into hermitage and do everything in your power to avoid human contact for the rest of your life? You are quite confident that you would not be impressed with what you would find in the minds of those you encounter. This is largely, if not entirely, due to the fact that you are intimately familiar with the contents of your *own* mind, and as you are a member of the same species as these persons you encounter, you are fairly confident that the human mind is, in most cases, an ugly place. Perhaps this generalization from your own case is unwarranted. One sample, after all, is a weak foundation for a claim about all of humanity, or even the general preponderance thereof. On the other hand, a wolf is a wolf, is a wolf. Is it not so? Persons are more complex than wolves, and they manifest in a wider array of permutations, but you are a member of a species, and the essence of the species is present in each of its members. Were it not so, could they all be members of the same species? The talking apes all share an essence. Some identify this shared essence as *reason*. Maybe.

1As for you, you were dead in your trespasses and sins, 2in
which you used to walk when you conformed to the ways of
this world and of the ruler of the power of the air, the spirit
who is now at work in the sons of disobedience. 3At one time
we all lived among them, fulfilling the cravings of our flesh
and indulging its desires and thoughts. Like the rest, we were
by nature children of wrath.

4But because of His great love for us, God, who is rich in
mercy, 5made us alive with Christ, even when we were dead
in our trespasses. It is by grace you have been saved! 6And
God raised us up with Christ and seated us with Him in the
heavenly realms in Christ Jesus, 7in order that in the coming
ages He might display the surpassing riches of His grace,
demonstrated by His kindness to us in Christ Jesus.

Ephesians 2

Beware debt. This is not only a matter of finances, but also a matter of owing favors or obeisance to the wrong people, powers, and organizations. When you owe anything to another person, you are, to that extent, under that person's thumb and subject to various forms of influence. This condition is a not-too-distant cousin of slavery. What is it that you are incapable of securing for yourself, and that is also necessary for survival? If you borrow money to purchase anything that you do not need, you are a fool and a child. Why subject yourself to usury at the hands of a lender, in order to attain something without which you can readily make do? When you ask for a favor, you are admitting weakness and an inability to accomplish some task by virtue of your own efforts. What do you want with those things that you cannot get for yourself and on your own? Self-sufficiency obviates the need for such favors. Keep your needs and desires as simple as possible, and you should have no need to borrow money, ask for favors, or owe anyone anything. Do not enslave yourself to others, or to circumstances, because you are too weak to restrain yourself and adhere to the dictates of reason. Profligacy is weakness.

> 13 In the fourteenth year of the reign of Hezekiah, Sennacherib
> king of Assyria attacked and captured all the fortified cities
> of Judah. 14 So Hezekiah king of Judah sent word to the king
> of Assyria at Lachish, saying, "I have done wrong; withdraw
> from me, and I will pay whatever you demand from me."
>
> And the king of Assyria exacted from Hezekiah king of Judah
> three hundred talents of silver and thirty talents of gold.
> 15 Hezekiah gave him all the silver that was found in the house
> of the LORD and in the treasuries of the royal palace.
>
> 16 At that time Hezekiah stripped the gold with which he had
> plated the doors and doorposts of the temple of the LORD,
> and he gave it to the king of Assyria.
>
> 2 Kings 18

You cannot be insulted or offended without your complicity. This is practically a trivial truth, it ought to be obvious, and you would expect it to be an uncontroversial claim, but it has, somehow, escaped the notice of the bulk of the masses. How many times have you heard complaints that so-and-so "made" some idiot angry, or "hurt" some weakling's feelings? It becomes impossible to take such persons seriously, does it not? The whining, the griping, the petulance, the whole cacophony of grievance emerges from the pit of the most ignominious depths of the corrupt soul of humanity. The insistence that you *must* be respected, that you *must* be treated fairly, that you *must* be loved, that you *must* be regarded as an equal, all of this is vapid stupidity. No one has any obligation to *regard* you at all. Yet you allow yourself, time and time again, to be thrown off balance by an unkind remark, or a perceived slight. You allow your serenity to be undercut by a sneer or a laugh intended at your expense. Can you not disregard such matters, as they are clearly not within your control and, therefore, clearly none of your business? If not, then waste your life accumulating one grievance after another. Perhaps your last words will be, "It wasn't fair!" Let that be your epitaph.

8 How can I give you up, O Ephraim?
How can I surrender you, O Israel?
How can I make you like Admah?
How can I treat you like Zeboiim?
My heart is turned within Me;
My compassion is stirred!
9 I will not execute the full fury of My anger;
I will not turn back to destroy Ephraim.
For I am God and not man—
the Holy One among you—
and I will not come in wrath.
10 They will walk after the LORD;
He will roar like a lion.
When He roars,
His children will come trembling from the west.
11 They will come trembling like birds from Egypt
and like doves from the land of Assyria.
Then I will settle them in their homes,
declares the LORD.

Hosea 11

When has anger, when has rage ever done you any good? What can you accomplish while enraged that you cannot accomplish when your mind is clear and governed by reason? Again and again you have made a fool of yourself under the influence of anger. You speak words that you later regret. You do things that cause you subsequent embarrassment, and you know that you *deserve* to feel small. Indeed, you have had occasion to conjure up some reason to become irate when, in reality, nothing has happened. What kind of warped mind invents phony justifications for befuddling itself with imaginary malice, or delusions of mistreatment? It is as if you *enjoy* being angry. Some part of you actually *does* derive a perverse form of pleasure from the experience of (allegedly) righteous indignation. This is petty. This is irrational. This is absolutely contrary to your professed values, and the pursuit of wisdom and virtue that you claim as your overarching purpose. Are you a charlatan? Are you false at heart? Perhaps you just like the idea of lofty goals, but lack the fortitude for the genuine pursuit thereof. Phony.

> [10]But the following among all the teeming life and creatures
> in the water are detestable to you: everything in the seas or
> streams that does not have fins and scales. [11]They shall be an
> abomination to you; you must not eat their meat, and you
> must detest their carcasses. [12]Everything in the water that
> does not have fins and scales shall be detestable to you.
>
> [13]Additionally, you are to detest the following birds, and they
> must not be eaten because they are detestable: the eagle, the
> bearded vulture, the black vulture, [14]the kite, and any kind
> of falcon; [15]every kind of raven; [16]the ostrich, the night hawk,
> the gull, and any kind of hawk; [17]the little owl, the cormorant,
> the great owl, [18]the white owl, the desert owl, the osprey, [19]the
> stork, and any kind of heron; the hoopoe and the bat.
>
> Leviticus 11

The fact that a particular state of affairs is none of your business does not preclude your capacity to render judgment in the matter. If you know a man is cheating on his wife, you are free to disapprove. Indeed, you are *obligated* to disapprove. You may not have any obligation to tell the wife, you may not be in a proper position to castigate the man for his misbehavior, and you may not have any rational justification for being upset in the least, but are at liberty to acknowledge that adultery is inappropriate. You may, perhaps, be inclined to refer to it as a *sin*. In any event, you know that you *will not* participate in any form of similar behavior. This illustrates the necessity of rendering judgment. You need not attempt to impose your values on anyone else, but you are always obligated to *adhere* to your root values. *Your* behavior is *always* your business. Your cognitive tendencies are *always* proper objects of your introspection and your attention. Govern yourself as best you can, and leave others to their own self-rectification, or vice. Do not *impose* your views needlessly.

1 I will sing of Your loving devotion and justice;
to You, O LORD, I will sing praise.

2 I will ponder the way that is blameless—
when will You come to me?
I will walk in my house with integrity of heart.
3 I will set no worthless thing before my eyes.
I hate the work of those who fall away;
it shall not cling to me.
4 A perverse heart shall depart from me;
I will know nothing of evil.

5 Whoever slanders his neighbor in secret,
I will put to silence;
the one with haughty eyes and a proud heart,
I will not endure.
6 My eyes will be on the faithful of the land,
that they may dwell with me;
he who walks in the way of integrity
shall minister to me.

Psalm 101

Those who fight the righteous battle, those who place life and limb at risk for noble purposes, those are the people who deserve your admiration and respect. Do you have it in you to put your life on the line for the sake of defending the innocent, or for the preservation of your family, or for any purpose that would be pleasing to a just God (if there *is* a just God)? Pacifism is not, perhaps, an indefensible position, but anyone who is unwilling to resort to violence even in defense of self, family, community, or the innocent, owes an argument in support of the decision to refrain from the fight. The burden of proof must be borne by those who claim that violence is *always* forbidden, or that it is a vice in *every* case imaginable. What is the case for allowing the victimization of your family, friends, or colleagues at the hands of miscreants, especially if you possess the wherewithal to intervene and eliminate the threat? Indeed, there may be *words* that warrant resort to "the sweet reason of the fist." Some speech acts are not to be tolerated. What does the pacifist's wife and children think of the "principles" that permit them to suffer mistreatment needlessly?

8When Asa heard these words and the prophecy of Azariah
son of Oded the prophet, he took courage and removed the
detestable idols from the whole land of Judah and Benjamin
and from the cities he had captured in the hill country of
Ephraim. He then restored the altar of the LORD that was in
front of the portico of the LORD's temple. 9And he assembled
all Judah and Benjamin, along with those from the tribes of
Ephraim, Manasseh, and Simeon who had settled among
them, for great numbers had come over to him from Israel
when they saw that the LORD his God was with him.

2 Chronicles 15

Do not say anything that you do not believe to be true, and do everything within reason to discover the truth, whatever the facts may be. Once you have made a determination as to the facts of any case, and once you have assessed the wisdom of speaking the truth on any given occasion (as opposed to maintaining silence), you *must* state the truth, even if doing so will cost you dearly. The world is filled with much more than enough prevarication as it is. You have no business contributing to its increase. Those who cannot stomach the truth are not, therefore, entitled to avoid encountering it. There is no such thing as a *right* to avoid unpleasant facts. In any event, the truth will not remain hidden from everyone forever. This is the case with, at least, *some* truths. Those truths that are inherently unknowable are, *a fortiori*, not knowable by *you*. So, you cannot be obligated to speak about these subjects. When you believe you know the truth, and when the truth is worth stating, however, if you refrain from speaking it, you will have diminished yourself, and you will deserve the guilty conscience and feeling of cowardice that are bound to ensue. Do not choose to "die a thousand deaths." Once is enough.

27 Why do you say, O Jacob,
and why do you assert, O Israel,
"My way is hidden from the LORD,
and my claim is ignored by my God"?
28 Do you not know?
Have you not heard?
The LORD is the everlasting God,
the Creator of the ends of the earth.
He will never grow faint or weary;
His understanding is beyond searching out.
29 He gives power to the faint
and increases the strength of the weak.
30 Even the youths may faint and grow weary,
and young men stumble and fall.
31 But those who wait upon the LORD
will renew their strength;
they will mount up with wings like eagles;
they will run and not grow weary;
they will walk and not faint.

Isaiah 40

Fatigue is not a sufficient excuse for a moral failure. You may be too tired to do one more pushup, or to run one more lap, but there is no such thing as being too tired to avoid lying, or too tired to behave respectfully toward someone who is deserving of your respect. You are not to cite a poor night's sleep as a justification for irresponsible behavior, or for cruelty that is unwarranted, or for disinterest in your central purposes and your pursuit of an ever more virtuous character. How much energy does it take to tell the truth? Certainly, it does not take more to tell the truth than it does to lie, especially given the energy it almost always takes to conceal the lie. Rational judgment may take more energy, at least in some cases, than does irrational, haphazard decision-making unguided by your reason, but that does not absolve you of the responsibility of trying your best to make the most reasonable and well informed decision you can. There is no such thing as being too worn-out to be decent and honorable. Do not fabricate nonsensical rationalizations. Have more self-respect than that.

18 If a man has a stubborn and rebellious son who does not obey
his father and mother, or listen to them when disciplined,
19 his father and mother are to lay hold of him and bring him
to the elders of his city, to the gate of his hometown, 20 and say
to the elders, "This son of ours is stubborn and rebellious; he
does not obey us. He is a glutton and a drunkard."

21 Then all the men of his city will stone him to death. You
must purge the evil from among you, and all Israel will hear
and be afraid.

Deuteronomy 21

What do you know about your heritage? Consider your ancestors from more than three or four generations back. You know virtually nothing about them. About earlier forebears, you know less still. Keep this in mind any time you find yourself fretting about "your" nation or "your" culture changing in ways that you regard as less than wholesome. How wholesome were your ancestors? How much did *they* change the regions into which they moved or migrated? You cannot know the answers to these questions. As for questions about the future evolution, or devolution, of your nation and its culture, you cannot be particularly confident about any suggested answers. Some, clearly, seem far more likely outcomes than do others. There is, at present, *no* evidence to indicate that your future self will exist in a more ennobling environment than you do now, but there is not that much to admire about your culture at present either, is there? If things go from bad to worse, as seems likely, remember that you are obligated to avoid declining along with them. Be responsible for *yourself*. The rest is not up to you.

13 For You formed my inmost being;
You knit me together in my mother's womb.
14 I will praise You,
for I am fearfully and wonderfully made.
Marvelous are Your works,
and I know this very well.
15 My frame was not hidden from You
when I was made in secret,
when I was woven together
in the depths of the earth.
16 Your eyes saw my unformed body;
all my days were written in Your book
and ordained for me
before one of them came to be.

Psalm 139

The reclusive life has much to recommend it. The lengthy spans of time without the distracting influence of other people has to be conducive to clearer thinking, less stress, and fewer causes for anger or enervation. Concerns about your appearance, though they are generally irrational and misguided under most circumstances, are all but precluded from arising where you are confident that no other persons can see you. Similarly, efforts at personal hygiene can be kept to the minimum required to maintain your health, but you can jettison all thoughts of body odor, bad breath, or the occasional blemish on your skin. These concerns should *never* be of any great significance to you, but in seclusion, they should fade away entirely. What hermit ever worried about passing gas? Most importantly, the lifestyle of the recluse affords a simplicity that is almost impossible to maintain in the presence of other people, their prying eyes, and their inquiring minds. Though you *should not* allow such matters to unsettle you, they often do. Until you improve to the point that other persons cause you no distress, it is advisable to take leave of them every so often. Perhaps you ought to take leave of them altogether.

November

14 Then the LORD raised up against Solomon an adversary,
Hadad the Edomite, from the royal line of Edom.

15 Earlier, when David was in Edom, Joab the commander of
the army had gone to bury the dead and had struck down
every male in Edom. 16 For Joab and all Israel had stayed there
six months, until he had killed every male in Edom. 17 But
Hadad, still just a young boy, had fled to Egypt, along with
some Edomites who were servants of his father.

1 Kings 11

Adversaries are not to be taken lightly, they are not to be disdained, and they are not to be resented. In the absence of an adversary, what are you supposed to do with your competitive spirit, and your desire to test yourself in a manner that requires another human being contending against you? It is all well and good to work out your body in the gym, and to train yourself to contend against environmental conditions, but another person wrestling against you, throwing punches and kicks at you, or matching wits with you in the context of a debate, a courtroom, or a contest of some kind, simply cannot be replicated by any struggle against inorganic matter. You need to look your adversary in the eyes, and to feel the force of that adversarial mind and spirit directed against you. Learn to appreciate those who contend against you. The more vigorously they work against you, the more you ought to appreciate and respect their efforts. The fighters are worthy of your respect. Even those who fight for ignoble causes can exhibit courage and fortitude in doing so. There is virtue in struggle. There is virtue in courage. There is virtue in perseverance.

> 11 Beloved, I urge you, as foreigners and exiles, to abstain
> from the desires of the flesh, which war against your soul.
> 12 Conduct yourselves with such honor among the Gentiles
> that, though they slander you as evildoers, they may see your
> good deeds and glorify God on the day He visits us.
>
> 13 Submit yourselves for the Lord's sake to every human
> institution, whether to the king as the supreme authority, 14 or
> to governors as those sent by him to punish evildoers and
> praise well-doers. 15 For it is God's will that by doing good
> you should silence the ignorance of foolish men.
>
> 1 Peter 2

It is time to reduce your emotional attachments to anything that could cause disappointment, and to anyone who could behave in such a fashion as to prove enervating, were the emotional attachment to persist. In this manner, you are to become a "small package," and diminish your potential exposure to psychological distress. You are old enough to understand that people, and the institutions that they create, are bound to disappoint—if you allow yourself to be disappointed by their behaviors or failures. Even the noblest human constructs eventually become debased, filthy, and vile. It seems as if there is something like a moral equivalent of the law of entropy. Everything becomes more disordered and repugnant over time. None of this is cause for despair, as long as you decline to allow the world to undermine your equanimity. Regard all things that your fellow talking apes construct as already corrupt beyond repair, from its very inception. In this way, you will not be disappointed when the inevitable occurs. Let the entirety of Western Civilization collapse—and let this be *nothing* to you.

5 Wake up, you drunkards, and weep;
wail, all you drinkers of wine,
because of the sweet wine,
for it has been cut off from your mouth.
6 For a nation has invaded My land,
powerful and without number;
its teeth are those of a lion,
and its fangs are those of a lioness.
7 It has laid waste My grapevine
and splintered My fig tree.
It has stripped off the bark and thrown it away;
the branches have turned white.

Joel 1

Is there no sense of urgency attendant upon the relentless approach of your own death? If death is the end of you, if there is no post-mortem persistence of the self, then you have *very* little time left, and you certainly have *no* time at all to waste—but you keep wasting your time. You spend hours engaged in activities that provide neither edification nor progress toward any useful goal. How many episodes of some ridiculous game show have contributed to making you a better person? None! How many movies have you watched only to conclude that your time would have been better-spent whittling soap into the shape of a duck? How many hours have you thrown away debating interlocutors who were clearly not susceptible to reason, and clearly disinterested in the truth? You may as well have spent that time banging your forehead against the nearest wall. Finally, how much of your limited, vital energy has been given over to frustration, anger, and despair over external events and conditions that have *nothing* to do with your central moral and intellectual purposes, and over which you exercise precisely *no* control whatsoever? If you witnessed someone else behaving this way, you would laugh and regard that person as a dimwit. Well... guess what.

3 You dismiss the day of calamity
and bring near a reign of violence.
4 You lie on beds inlaid with ivory,
and lounge upon your couches;
You dine on lambs from the flock
and calves from the stall.
5 You improvise songs on the harp like David
and invent your own musical instruments.
6 You drink wine by the bowlful
and anoint yourselves with the finest oils,
but you fail to grieve
over the ruin of Joseph.

7 Therefore, you will now go into exile
as the first of the captives,
and your feasting and lounging
will come to an end.

Amos 6

Another friend has died. Another member of the family has "shuffled off this mortal coil," and done so unexpectedly. You have grieved again. Can you not see that this is the way of things? The way of all flesh is manifest yet again. At some point, you really have to stop being surprised by the inevitable, the obvious, and the ubiquitous decrees of nature. This most recent case will, as you well know, *not* be the last. Did the grieving do you any good? Perhaps it did. Perhaps there is some cathartic benefit to it. It may have been, somehow, beneficial to others who loved the deceased. Do not, for this reason, persist in it for too long, or indulge in it in some overwrought fashion. Give death its due, gather your wits and your fortitude, and move forward. The dead have either gone on to some other place, some other mode of being, or they have ceased to exist altogether. In any event, your distress does them no good. Unless you acquire the power of resurrection, you would do well to turn your mind and your energy to other endeavors. Leave the dead in peace, and get back to the business of life while you still can.

17 After Jesus had left the crowd and gone into the house, His
disciples inquired about the parable.

18 "Are you still so dull?" He asked. "Do you not understand?
Nothing that enters a man from the outside can defile him,
19 because it does not enter his heart, but it goes into the
stomach and then is eliminated." (Thus all foods are clean.)

20 He continued: "What comes out of a man, that is what
defiles him. 21 For from within the hearts of men come evil
thoughts, sexual immorality, theft, murder, adultery, 22 greed,
wickedness, deceit, debauchery, envy, slander, arrogance,
and foolishness. 23 All these evils come from within, and these
are what defile a man."

Mark 7

More and more, you find that you want less and less to do with contemporary cultural developments, and the persons driving the changes in your society, and the realms of media, social networking, or the "creative" industries. So much of what passes for "art" today is, in reality, pretense erected atop nonsense, all of which is shrouded in dull mediocrity. The practice of "giving the people what they want," is bound to result in mountains of garbage—both literally and figuratively. The landfills blossom with the detritus of generations who have been taught that conspicuous consumption is obligatory, the oceans teem with the runoff from a factory farming system that feeds the obese beyond the dreams of gustatory avarice, and the airwaves and Internet explode with mind-deadening and soul-numbing dreck, the likes of which would have resulted in imprisonment or exile for its creators in virtually any earlier age, anywhere on the face of the planet. You live in the era of excess, and the age of decay. All around you, your fellow talking primates exhibit their collective and individual psychoses. Remember, you are one of them. Have a nice day. Thoughts and prayers to the families of the victims of avarice... are thoughts and prayers wasted. Enjoy.

6 "He has made me a byword to the people;
I am the one in whose face they spit.
7 My eyes have grown dim with grief,
and my whole body is but a shadow.
8 The upright are appalled at this,
and the innocent are stirred against the godless.
9 Yet the righteous will hold to his way,
and the one with clean hands will grow stronger.
10 But come back and try again, all of you.
For I will not find a wise man among you.

11 My days have passed; my plans are broken off—
even the desires of my heart.
12 They have turned night into day
and have made light seem near in the face of darkness.
13 If I look for Sheol as my home,
if I spread out my bed in darkness,
14 and say to corruption, 'You are my father,'
and to the worm, 'My mother,' or 'My sister,'
15 where then is my hope?
Who can see any hope for me?
16 Will it go down to the gates of Sheol?
Will we go down together into the dust?"

Job 17

Even amid the stupidity of this fallen world, and even in the face of a deteriorating culture, you must still learn to practice gratitude for *all* of the life you have experienced to this point, and all of the life yet to come. Who are *you* to question the way of things? If there is a Creator and Designer of the cosmos, then you are in no position to complain about a world that the Creator had no obligation to offer you, or to grouse about a life that you never earned. If there is no Creator, and the universe is a self-existing, self-regulating, and homogeneous system, existing as a brute fact without explanation, then your discontent cannot be directed at anything other than the world itself. What sort of object is it at which you direct your complaint then? Do you expect a response? Do you imagine that you are entitled to a better life? From what, from whom, and on what basis, do you claim any such entitlement? The blind laws of nature owe you nothing. Matter and energy behave as they do, as they *must*. You are nothing more than a product of chance, natural processes, and a series of coincidences. Breathe in, breathe out, seek the best life you can find, and stop your whimpering.

15 I, Daniel, was grieved in my spirit, and the visions in my
mind alarmed me. 16 I approached one of those who stood by,
and I asked him the true meaning of all this.

So he told me the interpretation of these things: 17 "These four
great beasts are four kings who will arise from the earth. 18 But
the saints of the Most High will receive the kingdom and
possess it forever—yes, forever and ever."

19 Then I wanted to know the true meaning of the fourth
beast, which was different from all the others—extremely
terrifying—with iron teeth and bronze claws, devouring,
crushing, and trampling underfoot whatever was left. 20 I also
wanted to know about the ten horns on its head and the other
horn that came up, before which three of them fell—the horn
whose appearance was more imposing than the others, with
eyes and with a mouth that spoke words of arrogance. 21 As
I watched, this horn was waging war against the saints and
prevailing against them, 22 until the Ancient of Days arrived
and pronounced judgment in favor of the saints of the Most
High, and the time came for them to possess the kingdom.

Daniel 7

The absurdity of the human condition, and the particular absurdity of *your* life, is not to be dismissed or ignored. This is not absurdity in the sense of meaninglessness, although it *could* be that as well, but it is the absurdity of a general helplessness with respect to understanding what, if anything, you are supposed to be doing, why it matters, and the circumstance of being utterly dwarfed by the vastness of time and space. You are like a flea trying to figure out whether you do or do not live on a dog, what purpose the dog serves (if it exists at all), and what your life will have amounted to after the dog has gone to "that big farm upstate," and your life has been forgotten by all the other fleas. Indeed, the flea may have the better of this deal. It can, after all, actually *experience* the dog, though it does not understand that it does so. What does your experience reveal to you? What you see, hear, and feel is a strange mixture of joy, pain, anxiety, boredom, exhilaration, and confusion. You ask yourself, "What does it all *mean*?" You don't know the answer, and you suspect that you never will. The flea does not trouble itself with such questions.

5Although you are fully aware of this, I want to remind you
that after Jesus had delivered His people out of the land
of Egypt, He destroyed those who did not believe. 6And
the angels who did not stay within their own domain but
abandoned their proper dwelling—these He has kept in
eternal chains under darkness, bound for judgment on that
great day. 7In like manner, Sodom and Gomorrah and the
cities around them, who indulged in sexual immorality and
pursued strange flesh, are on display as an example of those
who sustain the punishment of eternal fire.

8Yet in the same way, these dreamers defile their bodies,
reject authority, and slander glorious beings. 9But even the
archangel Michael, when he disputed with the devil over
the body of Moses, did not presume to bring a slanderous
judgment against him, but said, "The Lord rebuke you!"
10These men, however, slander what they do not understand,
and like irrational animals, they will be destroyed by the
things they do instinctively. 11Woe to them! They have
traveled the path of Cain; they have rushed headlong into
the error of Balaam; they have perished in Korah's rebellion.

Jude 1

Immanuel Kant argued that using another person as a "mere means," or undermining that person's voluntary, fully informed consent, constituted the *sine qua non* of evil. Persons, as Kant understood them, are rational, autonomous beings with free will, and to treat them as if they lacked any of those qualities is to treat them as implements, or as tools that have only utility value. How many of the talking apes that you have met satisfy those Kantian criteria? It seems that most people, at best, *lapse* into rationality on the odd occasion. The rest of the time, it is difficult to make the case that reason has a great deal to do with their words or actions. It is, perhaps, even more difficult to determine the degree to which humans tend to be autonomous. If anything, most of them seem to jettison their autonomy any time that they suspect it may entail actual responsibility for their behavior. Autonomy is held up and prized when there is some success or some accomplishment afoot. In the face of failure or vicious behavior, it is nowhere to be found. Finally, what exactly *is* free will, given that we are all embedded in a universe that appears to be entirely governed by causal determinism? Perhaps Kant was a bit overly enamored of the human species, and the allegedly wondrous capacities thereof. You do well to get through a full day without flinging your feces.

23"This is blood!" they exclaimed. "The kings have clashed
swords and slaughtered each other. Now to the plunder,
Moab!"

24But when the Moabites came to the camp of Israel, the
Israelites rose up and attacked them, and they fled before
them. So the Israelites invaded their land and struck down
the Moabites. 25They destroyed the cities, and each man threw
stones on every good field until it was covered. They stopped
up every spring and cut down every good tree. Only Kir-
haraseth was left with stones in place, but men with slings
surrounded it and attacked it as well.

2 Kings 3

How much of your experience, and how much of your assessment of the nature of your fellow creatures, should you pass over in silence? What is to be said, usefully, when you hear or read about some ancient feud that erupts, yet again, in an act, or series of acts, that culminate in the death of thousands? To call such events "tragic," or to refer to the acts as "atrocities," or to pronounce guilt and innocence in the matter, all this seems so utterly useless. Indeed, doing so simply adds to the ever-growing litany of grievances, stokes the fires of hatred, and encourages more carnage. Your opinions are unlikely to be embraced by anyone who did not have the same antecedent biases that determine your judgment in these kinds of cases. Those whose biases incline them in the opposite direction are never going to be swayed by any words, any argument, or any evidence you can command. As for those who have no preexisting biases (and you have not, to your knowledge, encountered anyone apart from the ignorant or uninterested masses unburdened by bias), what is gained by drawing them nearer to your worldview as opposed to that held by the antagonists on the other side of the dispute? All talk in this arena is just so much shouting into the void, and congratulating your ego for being less foolish than those bellowing in the other direction. Shut up, already. Your words can do no good.

1 Concerning Moab, this is what the LORD of Hosts, the God of Israel, says:

"Woe to Nebo,
for it will be devastated.
Kiriathaim will be captured and disgraced;
the fortress will be shattered and dismantled.
2 There is no longer praise for Moab;
in Heshbon they devise evil against her:
'Come, let us cut her off from nationhood.'
You too, O people of Madmen, will be silenced;
the sword will pursue you.
3 A voice cries out from Horonaim,
'Devastation and great destruction!'
4 Moab will be shattered;
her little ones will cry out.

5 For on the Ascent to Luhith
they weep bitterly as they go,
and on the descent to Horonaim
cries of distress resound over the destruction:
6 'Flee! Run for your lives!
Become like a juniper in the desert.'"

Jeremiah 48

Wear your scars and your bruises, your aches and your pains, and the other accumulated bodily damage, in the manner of a warrior. You are not, of course, an actual warrior, and you must never arrogate that status to any of your endeavors. It is the *real* warrior to whom that status is properly reserved. Nonetheless, you would do well to carry yourself as an active, voluntary participant in a life lived viscerally, and never present yourself to others, or regard yourself within the confines of your consciousness, as a victim, or as one who suffers unjustly. You deserve every bit of pain that befalls you. There is a way to escape it all, and you have not, as yet, chosen that way out. Do not complain of suffering if you have voluntarily chosen to remain in the place, and in the condition, in which suffering is well known to occur. Every moment of your life constitutes a decision to persist. Do not weep for the damages you have incurred, or for those yet to come. Withstand the buffeting and grinding of life in embodied form, be thankful for the opportunity to give this ride a whirl, and never complain of your fate. Either that… or end it.

6 Blessed be the LORD,
for He has heard my cry for mercy.
7 The LORD is my strength and my shield;
my heart trusts in Him, and I am helped.
Therefore my heart rejoices,
and I will thank Him with my song.

8 The LORD is the strength of His people,
a stronghold of salvation for His anointed.
9 Save Your people and bless Your inheritance;
shepherd them and carry them forever.

Psalm 28

When is the last time you set aside a moment to give thanks for those who grow the food that you eat? What of those who supply the security for which you rarely express thanks? Those who conceive, design, engineer, and manufacture the roads, the bridges, the buildings, the plumbing, the electrical apparatus, and the other infrastructure about which you understand virtually nothing, and upon which you depend for your survival, as well as for a life of luxury unknown to almost all of your ancestors, they seldom hear "thank you" from your lips. What an ingrate you are! You are like the weary traveler who shows up at a stranger's house, receives a free meal, free lodging for the night, and then leaves the next morning without so much as a tip of the hat to the homeowners. Do you believe that you are *entitled* to any of the largesse that you enjoy? Your efforts have produced *none* of it. Your very life is an entirely unearned benefit derived from a web of events stretching back to the Big Bang and the concatenation of causes and effects that followed. Can you experience anything other than gratitude for the world, and its unfolding, without which you would not even exist? No one respects an ungrateful lout.

> 22 Take notice, therefore, of the kindness and severity of God:
> severity to those who fell, but kindness to you, if you continue
> in His kindness. Otherwise you also will be cut off. 23 And if
> they do not persist in unbelief, they will be grafted in, for
> God is able to graft them in again. 24 For if you were cut from
> a wild olive tree, and contrary to nature were grafted into
> one that is cultivated, how much more readily will these, the
> natural branches, be grafted into their own olive tree!
>
> Romans 11

The concept of "the first day of the new year" is entirely a nonsensical human construct. The planet has completed one more rotation on its axis, and it continues to revolve around the sun, currently occupying a point in its orbit that is, in no way, objectively distinguishable from any other point on the orbit. The "first day of the new year" could just as easily have been associated with the first day of Spring, the first day of August, or any other day on the calendar. As for twelve o'clock "midnight," that particular moment is not unique. Much like money, the whole charade is simply made up. That does not make the construct useless. Calendars, clocks, and watches are implements without which modernity is nearly unthinkable. Of course, it seems to follow that modernity is, at least in part, predicated upon a nonsensical construct that could have been adjusted or altered in any number of directions. It is only a slight oversimplification to say that modernity is a fiction. This is nothing more than an era (*another* construct) cordoned off from the rest of history by chimerical inventions of human fancy. Man loves to pretend that he is the measure of all things. This is a bad habit.

6 This is the text of the letter that Tattenai the governor of
the region west of the Euphrates, Shethar-bozenai, and their
associates, the officials in the region, sent to King Darius.
7 The report they sent him read as follows:

To King Darius:

All peace.

8 Let it be known to the king that we went into the province of
Judah, to the house of the great God. The people are rebuilding
it with large stones, and placing timbers in the walls. This
work is being carried out diligently and is prospering in their
hands.

Ezra 5

From the observer's perspective, what is the difference between being polite, and *pretending* to be polite? What, for that matter, is the difference from the perspective of the agent who *is*, or who *pretends* to be, polite? Is there an "inner sneer" in the latter case? Perhaps this sneer is, somehow, available via introspection, but can you distinguish the presence of your own inner sneer from its absence—even after that ten thousandth greeting? At yet another social function, you may be introduced to three, ten, or twenty different people. You do your best, for the most part, to "be polite." How often is this mere pretense, and how often are your efforts sincere? Indeed, if you have to "make an effort," does this not indicate that there is something disingenuous about the entire affair? You enjoy meeting new people about as much as you enjoy contracting new viruses, and yet you are expected to smile, grip the far end of a proffered appendage, and state your name like a doll with a string pulled from the center of your back. How can this behavior lack the stench of pretense? Another silly, manufactured ritual of interaction haunts human affairs. Sad.

11 Why did I not perish at birth;
why did I not die as I came from the womb?
12 Why were there knees to receive me,
and breasts that I should be nursed?
13 For now I would be lying down in peace;
I would be asleep and at rest
14 with kings and counselors of the earth,
who built for themselves cities now in ruins,
15 or with princes who had gold,
who filled their houses with silver.
16 Or why was I not hidden like a stillborn child,
like an infant who never sees daylight?
17 There the wicked cease from raging,
and there the weary find rest.
18 The captives enjoy their ease;
they do not hear the voice of the oppressor.
19 Both small and great are there,
and the slave is freed from his master.

Job 3

The vague disquiet that periodically taps at the back of your brain is slightly more assertive today than it is on most other days. Do you know the cause? Is it merely a matter of brain chemistry? Is there some event on the horizon causing you a bit of increased anxiety? Perhaps this phenomenon has nothing to do with *you* at all, but you have tapped into some free-floating, generalized malaise of the *zeitgeist*. On the other hand, it may be that you just did not sleep particularly well last night, or you had something for breakfast that did not exactly agree with you. From the fact that some experience is available to your introspection, it does not follow that its origin, its etiology, or its explanation is equally available. Often, it is your own thoughts that prove most befuddling, and for which it is most difficult to pin down a rationale. It may be that you are just a little mentally ill, and you occasionally experience a conscious manifestation of the underlying psychological malady. This is not impossible, is it? Indeed, this explanation is at least as likely as any other. If something genuinely tragic happens today, take heart! It might mean you are *not* crazy.

1And I, in the first year of Darius the Mede, stood up to
strengthen and protect him.

2Now then, I will tell you the truth: Three more kings will
arise in Persia, and then a fourth, who will be far richer than
the others. By the power of his wealth, he will stir up everyone
against the kingdom of Greece.

3Then a mighty king will arise, who will rule with great
authority and do as he pleases. 4But as soon as he is established,
his kingdom will be broken up and parceled out toward the
four winds of heaven. It will not go to his descendants, nor
will it have the authority with which he ruled, because his
kingdom will be uprooted and given to others.

Daniel 11

The politicians are telling lies again today. In related news, water remains wet. Their dishonesty has ceased to be a source of consternation, and you struggle to take anything in the political realm seriously. The public knows that the politicians are lying; the politicians know that the public knows that they are lying, and the dance continues for no reason other than habit and, perhaps, lack of a viable alternative. Democracy is simply a ludicrous system for governing a nation. It is not, in fact, as Winston Churchill (or, perhaps, Richard M. Langworth) allegedly quipped, "the worst form of government, except for all the others," and it is simply not true that all other conceivable forms of government have been instantiated. No, it is a kind of cultural and intellectual inertia that keeps your nation, and the Western world, locked into this dismal suicide pact. All democracies accrue massive debt, because the masses eventually vote themselves so much public largesse, and also vote themselves so little responsibility for paying the price of that largesse, that a kind of Ponzi scheme is nearly inevitable. The masses always become fat, soft, weak, and sedentary. There is a collectivist rot at the heart of democracy, and no change of party gripping the levers of power is ever sufficient to forestall the slide into decadence and, ultimately, disaster. The masses just hope that the decline is slow enough to allow their individual deaths to precede the inevitable liquidation. At some point, this hope will be frustrated. For now, the citizens pretend not to notice that cliff toward which the culture trundles blindly. Ah, well. Try to enjoy the show.

December

1Then the word of the LORD came to me, saying, 2"Son of
man, you are living in a rebellious house. They have eyes to
see but do not see, and ears to hear but do not hear, for they
are a rebellious house.

3Therefore, son of man, pack your bags for exile. In broad
daylight, set out and go from your place to another as they
look on. Perhaps they will understand, though they are a
rebellious house. 4Bring out your baggage for exile by day, as
they look on. Then in the evening, as they look on, go out like
those who go into exile."

Ezekiel 12

The feeling of exile, of separation from what you once thought of as "your" culture, of existing apart from others, that feeling is particularly pronounced today, is it not? You look and listen as the various media blare away with whatever it is that passes for "news," at any given hour of any given day, and you feel no connection to *any* of it. It is as if the broadcasts originate from some distant galaxy, inhabited by soulless ghouls, desperate adolescents seeking attention, and withered phantoms that once strove to make something of their lives, but now await the sweet embrace of death, and do so under the influence of sedatives and pointless blather. Who *are* these people? What have they done to the world into which you were born? Are they all blind, deaf, and stupid, or have they actually concocted this bouillabaisse of pathologies and embarrassments on purpose? Inevitably, you will take a cognitive half-step back, consider the dying culture you behold, and you will realize that you are at least as much one of "them" as anyone else. Look at the gross product of *your* life's endeavors, and ask yourself what, if anything, warrants the pride of accomplishment or achievement. What do you find? Hold it up for all to see, and then let the general appraisal, your own included, wash over you. How hollow you feel at your core. You exiled yourself from the life that you could have lived, and you did it a long time ago. Do not issue complaints today.

58 If you are not careful to observe all the words of this
law which are written in this book, that you may fear this
glorious and awesome name—the LORD your God— 59 He
will bring upon you and your descendants extraordinary
disasters, severe and lasting plagues, and terrible and chronic
sicknesses. 60 He will afflict you again with all the diseases
you dreaded in Egypt, and they will cling to you.

61 The LORD will also bring upon you every sickness and
plague not recorded in this Book of the Law, until you are
destroyed. 62 You who were as numerous as the stars in the
sky will be left few in number, because you would not obey
the voice of the LORD your God.

Deuteronomy 28

If you *must* wreck your life and your character, make sure to refrain from taking others down with you. Perhaps you are entitled to throw your own life away in the pursuit of stupid, ignoble, and unhealthy aims, but you are a miserable creature indeed, if you corrupt others through your self-destructive endeavors. You are a coward and a weakling if you take the easy path of dissolution and moral degeneracy, but you are a far more foul and repugnant being if you coax others onto that same moribund path. The best and most reliable method, of course, for making certain that you do not lead others astray, is to keep *yourself* on the straight and narrow, avoid vice and corrupting influences, and set your sights on noble ideals and worthy goals. If you are unable or unwilling to pursue decency for its own sake, and if you lack sufficient self-respect to do so for the sake of your own enlightenment and liberation from degeneracy, you *must*, at the very least, do your best to move in the general direction of virtue if, for no other reason, than fulfilling your responsibility to avoid being a bad example and an evil influence upon others.

The best way to avoid metastasizing is to decline to allow your character to become a cancer in the first place.

14For this is what the LORD of Hosts says: "Just as I resolved
to bring disaster upon you when your fathers provoked Me
to anger, and I did not relent," says the LORD of Hosts, 15"so
now I have resolved to do good again to Jerusalem and Judah.
Do not be afraid. 16These are the things you must do: Speak
truth to one another, render true and sound decisions in your
gates, 17do not plot evil in your hearts against your neighbor,
and do not love perjury, for I hate all these things," declares
the LORD.

Zechariah 8

Evidently, you are now to add another item to the list of "Truths That Are To Remain Unspoken," and you are to acknowledge yet another fraud pervading the halls of the Academy, and besotting every media outlet that values political correctness more than it values honesty. This particular claim does not lie within your field of expertise, so it is inappropriate for you to comment upon it here. That might seem like you are just participating in the general cowardice, and perhaps you are, but the people who have devoted their adult lives and their careers to learning such theories and propositions, and marshaling evidence in their support, are the people upon whom the burden weighs most heavily (though few seem willing the shoulder that burden). Where there is trespass into the realm of claims about intellect, cognitive function, and its heritability, there can, apparently, be no such thing as rational, honest, evidence-based discussion, and there can be no theorizing outside the bounds of "good taste," as circumscribed by the ever-so-sensitive, and oh-so-enlightened thought police of the day. If the truth might upset some prevailing orthodoxies, then it is never to be recognized, and certainly not *publicly* recognized, as the truth. Why, there might be hurt feelings, after all. We cannot have *that*. No, it is better that the heavens should fall, than that the world might come to know an uncomfortable fact. People wonder why you are a misanthrope. Oh… no reason. Harrumph!

30"So if the boy is not with us when I return to your servant,
my father—his life is wrapped up in the boy's life—31when
he sees that the boy is not with us, he will die. Then your
servants will have brought the gray hair of your servant
our father down to Sheol in sorrow. 32Indeed, your servant
guaranteed the boy's safety to my father, saying, 'If I do not
return him to you, I will bear the guilt before you, my father,
all my life.'

33Now please let your servant stay here as my lord's slave, in
place of the boy. Let him return with his brothers. 34For how
can I go back to my father without the boy? I could not bear
to see the misery that would overwhelm him."

Genesis 44

When is the last time that you heard some clearly upstanding, moral stalwart offer the advice that you "should not be so judgmental"? This may well be *good* advice, and it may be wise to decline to cast aspersions, but it is almost never the best among us who prattle on about adjudicating immoral conduct, and ascribing proportional penalties. No, it is, almost invariably, those whose conduct cries out the loudest for condemnation who warn the rest of us that we ought not condemn so readily. Indeed, is it not precisely at those moments that *you* have felt most ashamed of your conduct, and those instances in which you were most humiliated at being caught, that you have experienced this defensive urge to warn against "casting the first stone"? It is when you have been up to no good that you become interested in reflexive forgiveness, is it not? No one responds in this manner to being judged a *hero*. Certainly, the "humble man" has frequently denied that his conduct should be regarded as heroic (at least out loud, and in public), but no one ever did so with an attitude of righteous indignation. No one ever thundered, "How *dare* you call me that?" No, the rejection of a plaudit is always good-natured, gentle, and matter of fact. Not so when we are caught red-handed, doing the devil's work. Is this interesting, or is it precisely what any rational adult ought to expect?

9But even the archangel Michael, when he disputed with
the devil over the body of Moses, did not presume to bring
a slanderous judgment against him, but said, "The Lord
rebuke you!" 10These men, however, slander what they do not
understand, and like irrational animals, they will be destroyed
by the things they do instinctively. 11Woe to them! They have
traveled the path of Cain; they have rushed headlong into the
error of Balaam; they have perished in Korah's rebellion.

Jude 1

Consider all the things that you do not want, all the issues about which you do not care, and all of the news of the day that does not move you in the least. How is it possible that so many can, apparently, concern themselves so deeply about matters to which you are *utterly* indifferent? It seems that your values are, once again, out of step with the values and interests of the culture within which you find yourself, somehow, embedded. It seems that you were born in the wrong place, at the wrong time, and placed among alien beings that you would, for the most part, prefer never to have encountered. Who *are* these people? What are they doing with their lives, and *why* should you care about any of them? It is as if someone is playing a joke on you, and the gag is the destruction of nearly everything that was once noble, decent, and worthy of admiration. Not much of a joke, really. Perhaps it is the Devil's sense of humor at work here. He *is* actually kind of a funny guy.

37 "Do not judge, and you will not be judged. Do not condemn,
and you will not be condemned. Forgive, and you will be
forgiven. 38 Give, and it will be given to you. A good measure,
pressed down, shaken together, and running over will be
poured into your lap. For with the measure you use, it will be
measured back to you."

39 Jesus also told them a parable: "Can a blind man lead a
blind man? Will they not both fall into a pit? 40 A disciple is
not above his teacher, but everyone who is fully trained will
be like his teacher.

41 Why do you look at the speck in your brother's eye, but
fail to notice the beam in your own eye? 42 How can you say,
'Brother, let me take the speck out of your eye,' while you
yourself fail to see the beam in your own eye? You hypocrite,
first take the beam out of your own eye, and then you will see
clearly to remove the speck from your brother's eye."

Luke 6

Take care when you mount your high horse, dummy. There are, without question, flaws, foibles, and sins enough for you to notice, comment upon, and warn against, but never lose sight of the fact that the malefactors you notice are members of *your* species, are related to you either directly or obliquely, and are components of the same current instantiation of humanity as *you*. In other words, a bit of hesitation before leaping to condemnation of the "imbeciles, liars, and losers" around you is almost certainly warranted. Have you never played the imbecile, either intentionally or by happenstance? Have you never told a lie? Have you lied *today*? Have you never failed at an important endeavor, or lost a competition that, at the time, mattered a great deal to you? The answers to all of those questions are, of course, blindingly obvious. You are free to engage in rational assessments of the behaviors you behold, indeed, a good case can be made that you are morally obligated to do so. If, however, you manage to convince yourself that you are inherently superior to those against whom you cast judgment, *then* you have fallen afoul of the wise advice to "judge not, lest ye be judged." The sin is not in the judgment, but rather in the presumption that you are *superior* to those whom you judge. Judgment is inevitable. Delusions of moral superiority are avoidable. Eschew them.

1 Now the whole world had one language and a common form
of speech. 2 And as people journeyed eastward, they found a
plain in the land of Shinar and settled there.

3 And they said to one another, "Come, let us make bricks and
bake them thoroughly." So they used brick instead of stone,
and tar instead of mortar.

4 "Come," they said, "let us build for ourselves a city with a
tower that reaches to the heavens, that we may make a name
for ourselves and not be scattered over the face of all the
earth."

5 Then the LORD came down to see the city and the tower
that the sons of men were building. 6 And the LORD said, "If
they have begun to do this as one people speaking the same
language, then nothing they devise will be beyond them.
7 Come, let Us go down and confuse their language, so that
they will not understand one another's speech."

8 So the LORD scattered them from there over the face of all
the earth, and they stopped building the city. 9 That is why
it is called Babel, for there the LORD confused the language
of the whole world, and from that place the LORD scattered
them over the face of all the earth.

Genesis 11

Consider the possibility, though you know it to be so remote as to border upon the impossible, of all "People of the Book" coming together, laying aside all past and present grievances between them, treating doctrinal differences as insignificant or, at the very least, unworthy of preventing the union of all devotees of the Abrahamic traditions, and taking up the cause of doing God's will as best they are able, and as best they may identify the nature of God's will. Imagine all Jews, Christians, and Muslims joining forces and working together to change the world, its cultures, and themselves, in a manner that they believe to be pleasing to the Lord. Even if there is no God, what force on this planet could possibly stand against the unified throngs of those who *believe* themselves to be pursuing noble and pious goals? The "Armies of Abraham" would be as close to invincible as any throng of mere mortals that the world has ever known. The "Nations of the Noahide" would be all but unstoppable. Does Allah condemn the sectarianism that forestalls the triumph of His people, or is this all part of the divine plan. The Tower of Babel was not, after all, a welcome development, according to scripture. Perhaps humankind, even those who claim to revere the Lord, cannot be trusted to manage the heights of power to which they are capable of ascending. Perhaps our reach exceeds our grasp. Perhaps God knows that He cannot trust us. Then again, humankind may just be an inveterate mess all on its own—without the need for divine intervention.

1 On another day, the sons of God came to present themselves
before the LORD; and Satan also came with them to present
himself before Him.

2 "Where have you come from?" said the LORD to Satan.

"From roaming through the earth," he replied, "and walking
back and forth in it."

3 Then the LORD said to Satan, "Have you considered My
servant Job? For there is no one on earth like him—blameless
and upright, fearing God and shunning evil. He still retains
his integrity, even though you incited Me against him to ruin
him without cause."

4 "Skin for skin!" Satan replied. "A man will give up all he
owns in exchange for his life. 5 But stretch out Your hand and
strike his flesh and bones, and he will surely curse You to
Your face."

Job 2

Might not the Devil of the scriptures be, primarily, a personification of human selfishness? The Devil tempts people to pursue selfish interests, and to ignore any and all overarching moral or social concerns. Perhaps the Devil is intended as part of a cautionary tale indicating the perils of selfishness, and the pervasive temptations to ignore the dictates of decency in the pursuit of ego gratification or the satisfaction of some bestial urge. The next time you notice an urge to satisfy a self-centered interest to the detriment of the rights, liberties, or fundamental personhood of other human beings, it might be useful to remind yourself that the Devil is tempting you. The Devil need not be an actual entity. Satan may be no more than a fictitious character in a narrative about a God that does not really exist. None of that undermines the practical value of identifying unhealthy, irrational, or otherwise inappropriate urges as manifestations of a malevolent being against whom your defenses ought always to be raised. It may be easier and more felicitous to associate the unsavory elements of the human character, and the unfortunate temptations of the human condition, with an external entity that can be more readily identified as a threat, than with an internal defective portion of the human self. It feels more natural to fight against a foe that is someone other than oneself.

24Then the LORD rained down brimstone and fire on Sodom
and Gomorrah—from the LORD out of the heavens. 25Thus
He destroyed these cities and the entire plain, including all
the inhabitants of the cities and everything that grew on the
ground.

26But Lot's wife looked back, and she became a pillar of salt.

27Early the next morning, Abraham got up and returned to
the place where he had stood before the LORD. 28He looked
down toward Sodom and Gomorrah and all the land of the
plain, and he saw the smoke rising from the land like smoke
from a furnace.

29So when God destroyed the cities of the plain, He remembered
Abraham, and He brought Lot out of the catastrophe that
destroyed the cities where he had lived.

Genesis 19

You will encounter deceit, stupidity, malice, incompetence, sloth, gluttony, and every other vice you can name, and you will encounter each of these nearly every day of your life. This does not justify any complaint whatsoever. You are not absolved of your obligation to live in accordance with reason, as best you are able, merely because so many people who appear to lack interest in doing likewise, or who lack the ability to do so surround you. Indeed, the more pervasive the vice, the greater the need for someone to attempt to counterbalance it by pursuing virtue. Perhaps this will have to be *you*. Of course, you have contributed more than your fair share to the unfortunate side of the ledger, have you not? Were you to take the time to list all of your vices, and all of the occasions upon which you have fallen into them, you would scarcely have time to do anything else. Your own defective nature must not be used as an excuse to cease your pursuit of improvement. Do not "throw up your hands" in despair and cry, "I am unworthy!" Of course you are! That is precisely the point, is it not? *Become* worthy. Even if all the world is on its way to Hell in the proverbial hand basket, and even if you see no way of getting yourself *out* of the hand basket, you are still obligated to struggle with all of your might to *try*. If there is some point to living a human life that does *not* involve trying to improve your character, that is a "point" devoid of purpose. Even if your life is nothing more than an accident, try to make it a beautiful one. Perhaps nobility can be derived even from catastrophe.

> 8Then Haman informed King Xerxes, "There is a certain
> people scattered and dispersed among the peoples of every
> province of your kingdom. Their laws are different from
> everyone else's, and they do not obey the king's laws; it is
> not in the king's best interest to tolerate them. 9If the king
> approves, let a decree be issued to destroy them, and I will
> deposit ten thousand talents of silver into the royal treasury
> to pay those who carry this out."
>
> Esther 3

All social engineering is doomed to failure. Any enterprise predicated upon the alleged "equality" or interchangeability of individuals, or of collectives identified by race, sex, ethnicity, religious affiliation, or any other parameter at all, is simply an attempt to elide the differences that, thankfully, are *not* universally and smoothly distributed across all populations. Real diversity, if it is to be valued, must not be homogenized out of existence by insisting that all individuals and collectives *must* share the same fundamental and overarching desires or beliefs. Thank God that vast swathes of the human race are very different from *you*. This phenomenon makes the human condition much more *interesting* than would a world filled with persons and groups that are all alike. *Vive la difference*! What is wrong with "social engineers" who seek to "manage" human affairs at every level, in every facet of interpersonal interaction, and in a manner that penetrates all the way into the cognitive states and worldviews of the entire populace? Who anointed these "Paladins of Equality," and where did any of them get the ridiculous idea that the rest of us wish to be "equals," or members of "one community," or anything of the sort? The Amish do not wish to live among the rest of us—and good for them! Can you blame them? Their "life apart" harms no one, and they seem quite content, arguably *more* content than the rest of us, to live in a separate and incommensurable fashion. What arrogance to wish to intervene in a way of life that harms the rest of us in no way whatsoever. Do not arrogate to yourself the authority to tell anyone else what to believe, how to live, or whom to respect and revere.

> 40 But if they will confess their iniquity and that of their
> fathers in the unfaithfulness that they practiced against Me,
> by which they have also walked in hostility toward Me—
> 41 and I acted with hostility toward them and brought them
> into the land of their enemies—and if their uncircumcised
> hearts will be humbled and they will make amends for their
> iniquity, 42 then I will remember My covenant with Jacob and
> My covenant with Isaac and My covenant with Abraham, and
> I will remember the land.
>
> 43 For the land will be abandoned by them, and it will enjoy
> its Sabbaths by lying desolate without them. And they will
> pay the penalty for their iniquity, because they rejected My
> ordinances and abhorred My statutes.
>
> Leviticus 26

In the absence of some form of covenant, and without someone or something to enforce the terms of that covenant, can human beings be trusted to live in an even minimally decent fashion? Some of them would probably be fairly trustworthy "on their own," so to speak, but would humanity at large be endurable with nothing binding them to a set of rules that are enforced by a threat of some type or other? Given the prevalence of crime, cruelty, war, and oppression even among those who *claim* to adhere to a covenant, you cannot help but project a far darker and more vicious world were the broad supposition of divine commands, and a commander who metes out justice even to those who can escape humanity's justice, to wither away. You also cannot help but notice that this supposition *is* withering away, and is commonly the object of contempt, derision, and unconcealed mockery. What follows the death of the belief in "the covenant" is going to be something very different from the world as it stands today. The current belief systems will be replaced with something else or, perhaps, with *nothing*. Show people *nothing*, and many of them are sure to make the most of it.

> 10 At that time Joshua turned back and captured Hazor and
> struck down its king with the sword, because Hazor was
> formerly the head of all these kingdoms. 11 The Israelites struck
> down everyone in Hazor with the sword, utterly destroying
> them. Nothing that breathed remained, and Joshua burned
> down Hazor itself.
>
> 12 Joshua captured all these kings and their cities and struck
> them down with the sword. He utterly destroyed them, as
> Moses the LORD's servant had commanded. 13 Yet Israel did
> not burn any of the cities built on their mounds, except Hazor,
> which Joshua burned.
>
> Joshua 11

Almost all people, almost anywhere on the face of the earth, at nearly every period in history, have been fascinated with fighting, with warfare, and with every sort of conflict imaginable. This is *not* a defect. Violence is bound to be fascinating. There is something primal about bloodshed that is probably ineradicable, at least for the foreseeable future, or until governments or corporations begin the neural "rewiring" of the populace, and a life devoid of any form of violence or conflict would be either the worst of all possible eventualities, or so wonderful that it lies somewhere beyond the powers of your imagination. You have not thrown a punch, a kick, or locked in a chokehold in genuine anger for some years now. Can you admit that you miss this? In some of your private moments, in the absence of any audience, when you have the luxury of brutally honest reflection, can you not feel the old urges, can you not recall or recapture the impulses that culminated in fisticuffs back in "the old days," before you became so abominably "sophisticated," and civilized? Without moral or visceral justification, violence is to be avoided, but when the cause presents itself, and when there is clear and present danger to yourself or someone you love, do not hesitate due to "civility." Your soul will suffer for it if you do.

1 The LORD is my shepherd;
I shall not want.
2 He makes me lie down in green pastures;
He leads me beside quiet waters.
3 He restores my soul;
He guides me in the paths of righteousness
for the sake of His name.
4 Even though I walk through the valley of the shadow of death,
I will fear no evil,
for You are with me;
Your rod and Your staff, they comfort me.

5 You prepare a table before me
in the presence of my enemies.
You anoint my head with oil;
my cup overflows.
6 Surely goodness and mercy will follow me
all the days of my life,
and I will dwell in the house of the LORD
forever.

Psalm 23

The Valley of the Shadow of Death is long, and the journey through it is frequently terrifying, but the alternative appears to be even less desirable. As long as you remain on your journey through the Valley, you must resist the urge to complain, to despair, or to become paralyzed with fear. You know the quickest way out of the Valley, but you have chosen to persist on your journey up to this point. You have read that you should "fear no evil," but you know that there is evil within you, and you *should* fear this inner malevolence. You *must* do everything within your power to keep the darkness inside of you under wraps, unless and until you have no viable alternative but to summon it to the surface. There *may* be saints traveling through the Valley, but *you* are not one of them. Perhaps some people do not need to cultivate a gentle and harmless frame of mind, as it comes to them quite naturally and without any specific cognitive effort. *You* are *not* such a person. Indeed, you are part of the shadow of the Valley, are you not? Are you not precisely the kind of thing that the fearful hold before their minds when gripped with anxiety? It is you, and people like you, that cast some of the Shadow, is it not? This is not a pleasant thought, but the truth of your condition is not always pleasant either. Do not extirpate the darkness from your character, but do not allow it to rule you either. The proper admixture is the healthiest goal. Find it.

17 Therefore, this is what the LORD says: You have not obeyed
Me; you have not proclaimed freedom, each man for his
brother and for his neighbor. So now I proclaim freedom
for you, declares the LORD—freedom to fall by sword, by
plague, and by famine! I will make you a horror to all the
kingdoms of the earth.

18 And those who have transgressed My covenant and have
not fulfilled the terms of the covenant they made before
Me, I will treat like the calf they cut in two in order to pass
between its pieces. 19 The officials of Judah and Jerusalem, the
court officials, the priests, and all the people of the land who
passed between the pieces of the calf, 20 I will hand over to
their enemies who seek their lives. Their corpses will become
food for the birds of the air and the beasts of the earth. 21 I
will hand Zedekiah king of Judah and his officials over to
their enemies who seek their lives, to the army of the king of
Babylon that had withdrawn from you.

Jeremiah 34

Never attempt to deprive *anyone* of freedom of speech and expression. There are times and places in which speaking is not appropriate, but there is no such thing as an idea that ought to be suppressed. Indeed, the worse the idea, the more malevolent the doctrine, the more vile the worldview, the more crucial it is that its expression is permitted. How are you to identify the worst human beings on the planet, if the most repugnant of the talking apes are not allowed to say the things that reveal the full depth and breadth of their morally diseased characters? Surely, you are better off knowing which apes are the ones against whom you and yours most need to erect cognitive battlements. What would be the motivation for proscribing "offensive" speech? Can it be anything other than cowardice, sloth, or stupidity? If you are not afraid to engage the filth in debate, there should be no hesitancy. If you are not too lazy to marshal the intellectual resources to expose the imbecile to the audience, there should be no reluctance to move forward. If you are not intellectually overmatched, you should have little difficulty defeating the lesser intellect. Only cowards, bullies, and imbeciles seek to stifle free speech. Do not become a coward, bully, or imbecile. Be an adult. Face your opponent and, if it is deserved, *humiliate* your opponent.

> 18 I testify to everyone who hears the words of prophecy in
> this book: If anyone adds to them, God will add to him the
> plagues described in this book. 19 And if anyone takes away
> from the words of this book of prophecy, God will take away
> his share in the tree of life and in the holy city, which are
> described in this book.
>
> 20 He who testifies to these things says, "Yes, I am coming
> soon." Amen. Come, Lord Jesus!
>
> 21 The grace of the Lord Jesus be with all the saints.
>
> Amen.
>
> Revelation 22

All things come to an end. The good, the bad, the ugly, the indifferent, and the things about which no evaluation can be offered in good faith, all of these pass away. You will lapse into silence, you will pass from this world, you will be forgotten, and the entirety of your existence will be swallowed up in the endless oceans of space and time. The human race will perish. Billions of years into the future, the universe will be devoid of life, and all of the stars will be gone. What is there to be done about any of this? You get to watch "the show" for a very short while. You get to play a tiny role in this play that you did not write, you do not direct, and your final scene occurs long before the script reaches its conclusion. Play your part as well as you are able. Do so with a full heart, and with nobility set as your goal. Perhaps you may hope for a "curtain call" (so to speak), but you cannot be certain that you will be called back out on stage. Nonetheless, you have no choice but to bet your life on the possibility. Pascal made the case that the manner in which you live your life *is* a wager, whether you like it or not. Your beliefs and your values guide you on your way. You are, of course, *far* from infallible in such matters. Here you are. Here, all about you, and within you, is the world as it stands. Now, get to work. Amen.

References

All quotations of scripture are taken from Bible Hub:
https://biblehub.com

Other Books by the Author

Meditations on Self-Discipline and Failure: Stoic Exercise for Mental Fitness (O-Books, ISBN 978 1 78535 587 5)
A Life Worth Living: Meditations on God, Death and Stoicism (O-Books, ISBN 978 1 78904 304 4)

SPIRITUALITY

O is a symbol of the world, of oneness and unity; this eye represents knowledge and insight. We publish titles on general spirituality and living a spiritual life. We aim to inform and help you on your own journey in this life.

If you have enjoyed this book, why not tell other readers by posting a review on your preferred book site?

Recent bestsellers from O-Books are:

Heart of Tantric Sex

Diana Richardson

Revealing Eastern secrets of deep love and intimacy to Western couples.

Paperback: 978-1-90381-637-0 ebook: 978-1-84694-637-0

Crystal Prescriptions

The A-Z guide to over 1,200 symptoms and their healing crystals

Judy Hall

The first in the popular series of eight books, this handy little guide is packed as tight as a pill-bottle with crystal remedies for ailments.

Paperback: 978-1-90504-740-6 ebook: 978-1-84694-629-5

Take Me To Truth

Undoing the Ego

Nouk Sanchez, Tomas Vieira

The best-selling step-by-step book on shedding the Ego, using the teachings of *A Course In Miracles*.

Paperback: 978-1-84694-050-7 ebook: 978-1-84694-654-7

The 7 Myths about Love...Actually!

The Journey from your HEAD to the HEART of your SOUL

Mike George

Smashes all the myths about LOVE.

Paperback: 978-1-84694-288-4 ebook: 978-1-84694-682-0

The Holy Spirit's Interpretation of the New Testament
A Course in Understanding and Acceptance
Regina Dawn Akers
Following on from the strength of *A Course In Miracles*, NTI teaches us how to experience the love and oneness of God.
Paperback: 978-1-84694-085-9 ebook: 978-1-78099-083-5

The Message of A Course In Miracles
A translation of the Text in plain language
Elizabeth A. Cronkhite
A translation of *A Course in Miracles* into plain, everyday language for anyone seeking inner peace. The companion volume, *Practicing A Course In Miracles*, offers practical lessons and mentoring.
Paperback: 978-1-84694-319-5 ebook: 978-1-84694-642-4

Rising in Love
My Wild and Crazy Ride to Here and Now, with Amma, the Hugging Saint
Ram Das Batchelder
Rising in Love conveys an author's extraordinary journey of spiritual awakening with the Guru, Amma.
Paperback: 978-1-78279-687-9 ebook: 978-1-78279-686-2

Thinker's Guide to God
Peter Vardy
An introduction to key issues in the philosophy of religion.
Paperback: 978-1-90381-622-6

Your Simple Path

Find Happiness in every step

Ian Tucker

A guide to helping us reconnect with what is really important in our lives.

Paperback: 978-1-78279-349-6 ebook: 978-1-78279-348-9

365 Days of Wisdom

Daily Messages To Inspire You Through The Year

Dadi Janki

Daily messages which cool the mind, warm the heart and guide you along your journey.

Paperback: 978-1-84694-863-3 ebook: 978-1-84694-864-0

Body of Wisdom

Women's Spiritual Power and How it Serves

Hilary Hart

Bringing together the dreams and experiences of women across the world with today's most visionary spiritual teachers.

Paperback: 978-1-78099-696-7 ebook: 978-1-78099-695-0

Dying to Be Free

From Enforced Secrecy to Near Death to True Transformation

Hannah Robinson

After an unexpected accident and near-death experience, Hannah Robinson found herself radically transforming her life, while a remarkable new insight altered her relationship with her father, a practising Catholic priest.

Paperback: 978-1-78535-254-6 ebook: 978-1-78535-255-3

The Ecology of the Soul

A Manual of Peace, Power and Personal Growth for Real People in the Real World

Aidan Walker

Balance your own inner Ecology of the Soul to regain your natural state of peace, power and wellbeing.

Paperback: 978-1-78279-850-7 ebook: 978-1-78279-849-1

Not I, Not other than I

The Life and Teachings of Russel Williams

Steve Taylor, Russel Williams

The miraculous life and inspiring teachings of one of the World's greatest living Sages.

Paperback: 978-1-78279-729-6 ebook: 978-1-78279-728-9

On the Other Side of Love

A woman's unconventional journey towards wisdom

Muriel Maufroy

When life has lost all meaning, what do you do?

Paperback: 978-1-78535-281-2 ebook: 978-1-78535-282-9

Practicing A Course In Miracles

A translation of the Workbook in plain language, with mentor's notes

Elizabeth A. Cronkhite

The practical second and third volumes of The Plain-Language *A Course In Miracles*.

Paperback: 978-1-84694-403-1 ebook: 978-1-78099-072-9

Quantum Bliss

The Quantum Mechanics of Happiness, Abundance, and Health

George S. Mentz

Quantum Bliss is the breakthrough summary of success and spirituality secrets that customers have been waiting for.

Paperback: 978-1-78535-203-4 ebook: 978-1-78535-204-1

The Upside Down Mountain

Mags MacKean

A must-read for anyone weary of chasing success and happiness – one woman's inspirational journey swapping the uphill slog for the downhill slope.

Paperback: 978-1-78535-171-6 ebook: 978-1-78535-172-3

Your Personal Tuning Fork

The Endocrine System

Deborah Bates

Discover your body's health secret, the endocrine system, and 'twang' your way to sustainable health!

Paperback: 978-1-84694-503-8 ebook: 978-1-78099-697-4

Readers of ebooks can buy or view any of these bestsellers by clicking on the live link in the title. Most titles are published in paperback and as an ebook. Paperbacks are available in traditional bookshops. Both print and ebook formats are available online.

Find more titles and sign up to our readers' newsletter at http://www.johnhuntpublishing.com/mind-body-spirit

Follow us on Facebook at https://www.facebook.com/OBooks/ and Twitter at https://twitter.com/obooks